CONTEMPORARY ILLUSTRATED BOOKS:
WORD AND IMAGE, 1967-1988

Donna Stein, guest curator

Essay by Donna Stein

A traveling exhibition organized and circulated by Independent Curators Incorporated, New York

ITINERARY

Franklin Furnace Archive, Inc.
New York, New York
12 January to 28 February 1990

Nelson-Atkins Museum of Art
Kansas City, Missouri
5 April to 3 June 1990

The University of Iowa Museum of Art
Iowa City, Iowa
8 February to 7 April 1991

This exhibition, tour, and catalogue
are made possible, in part, by a
grant from the National Endowment
for the Arts and contributions from
the ICI Exhibition Patrons Circle.
Additional funding has been provided
by The Cowles Charitable Trust.

LENDERS TO THE EXHIBITION

Diane and Martin Ackerman

The Arion Press, San Francisco

Galerie Baudoin Lebon, Paris

Mei-mei Berssenbrugge

Loriano Bertini

The Brooklyn Museum

Daniel Buren

Jim Dine

Editions Fanal, Basel

Vincent Fitz Gerald & Company, New York

The Grunwald Center for the Graphic Arts,
    University of California, Los Angeles

L'Inéditeur, Paris

Alex Katz

Landfall Press, Chicago and New York

The Limited Editions Club, Ltd., New York

Nancy and Edwin Marks

Milkweed Editions, Minneapolis

Richard Minsky

The Museum of Modern Art, New York

Pace Editions, New York

Petersburg, London and New York

Tom Phillips

Rose Art Museum, Brandeis University,
    Waltham, Massachusetts

Solo Press Inc., New York

Galerie Springer, Berlin

Fundació Antoni Tàpies, Barcelona

Sergio Tosi Stampatore, Paris and Rome

Richard Tuttle

Tyler Graphics Ltd., Mount Kisco, New York

Verlag 3, Zurich

Library of the Whitney Museum of
    American Art, New York

Stephen Wirtz Gallery, San Francisco

Irving Zucker Art Books, New York

INDEPENDENT CURATORS INCORPORATED

Independent Curators Incorporated,
New York, is a non-profit traveling
exhibition service specializing in
contemporary art. ICI's activities are
made possible, in part, by individual
contributions and grants from
foundations, corporations, and the
National Endowment for the Arts.

Editorial Consultant: Marybeth Sollins
Design: Russell Hassell
Composition: Trufont Typographers, Inc.
Lithography: The Studley Press

ACKNOWLEDGMENTS

This complex exhibition project has involved many contributors. Riva Castleman, Director of Prints & Illustrated Books, The Museum of Modern Art, New York, and Martha Wilson, Director of the Franklin Furnace Archive, Inc., New York, discussed the concept of the exhibition with me in its earliest stages and encouraged ICI to organize this twenty-one-year survey of *livres d'artiste*. But I am most indebted to Donna Stein, ICI's guest curator for the exhibition, for her research, dedication, and knowledge, and for her staunch loyalty to the project over the course of several years of preparation. On her behalf, I would like to thank Robert Rainwater, Curator of the Spencer Collection, The New York Public Library; Audrey Isselbacher, Kathleen Slavin, and Wendy Weitman, of the Department of Prints & Illustrated Books, The Museum of Modern Art, New York; May Castleberry, Librarian of the Whitney Museum of American Art; and Tony Zwicker.

The lenders to the exhibition have been extremely generous: I am grateful to each of them for parting with these extraordinary books. In addition, I would like to thank Vincent Fitz Gerald, Loriano Bertini, Richard Minsky, and Irving Zucker for their special contributions that aided Donna Stein and ICI's staff in the successful organization of the exhibition.

Many colleagues also assisted ICI's staff in the preparation of *Contemporary Illustrated Books*. In particular I would like to acknowledge the advice provided by Jane MacNicol, of Petersburg Press, Ruth Resnicow, of Solo Press Inc., and Susan Melton, Registrar of the Grunwald Center for the Graphic Arts, University of California, Los Angeles.

And, of course, I am keenly appreciative of the combined efforts of ICI's dedicated staff—Judith Olch Richards, Associate Director; Donna Harkavy, Exhibitions Coordinator; Jack Coyle, Registrar; Mary LaVigne, Development Associate/Newsletter Coordinator; Judy Gluck Steinberg, Associate Exhibitions Coordinator; Andrew Levy, Administrative Assistant; and Lise Holst, former Exhibitions Coordinator—each of whom played a key role in bringing *Contemporary Illustrated Books* into existence. In particular I would like to thank Donna Harkavy, Jack Coyle, and Judy Gluck Steinberg for the skill and devotion with which they produced the catalogue, located and obtained loans for specific works in the exhibition, and prepared the books and related materials for exhibition and travel. Judith Richards deserves our special thanks for her commitment to assuring the exhibition of its tour. Once again, I would also like to acknowledge and thank Russell Hassell for the design of another special ICI catalogue, and my sister Marybeth Sollins for her diligent research and editorial contributions.

I also extend my appreciation and gratitude to ICI's Board of Trustees for its continuing and loyal support of each of ICI's exhibitions.

Susan Sollins, Executive Director

Contemporary Illustrated Books:
Word and Image, 1967–1988

by Donna Stein

Contemporary Illustrated Books: Word and Image, 1967–1988 surveys recent developments in the long-lived genre of the *livre d'artiste*. The descriptive term *livre d'artiste* refers to books that contain original graphic work by artists with accompanying text, just as earlier in this century the term *livres de peintres* referred to such works by the "masters," most of whom were French painters and sculptors.[1] Books of this type are not so much *illustrated* as *created*,[2] and it would be misleading to describe the artists who create them only as illustrators.

The traditional approach to book design requires that an illustrated book "should be a harmonious combination of textual and pictorial elements, each significant, and each of *relatively equal importance*."[3] Thus, illustration has existed to enhance and complement text, to elucidate and amplify meaning—implying that the major role in book production lies with the author rather than the illustrator of the text. But, in the past century, the book "has become a major vehicle for artistic expression . . . in which the artist is not necessarily secondary to the author."[4]

Livres d'artiste develop from diverse sources. They may consist of works that illustrate pre-existing, already-published texts; they may represent a collaboration between artist and writer on previously unpublished material—or on a text specially written for the purpose of such collaboration—and, as such, are especially important as first editions; or they may be the artist's illumination of his or her own original written material. Some of the most successful illustrated books are unions in which author and artist are contemporaries, but have conceived their contributions separately. When combined, the works seem to become a totality greater than the original parts.

Artists often utilize existing historic or current literature. Some illustrate specific characters or events described in the texts; others create obscure images which nevertheless manage to connect with the pre-existing text.

Often it is the publisher who develops the idea for a book, having preconceived notions about the pairing of artist and writer and knowing almost instinctively which artists and writers will work well together. Some publishers however, introduce writers to artists only after long discussions and thoughtful consideration of an artist's ideas and work. Whether classic or contemporary, a text is often the crucial starting point, as it stimulates collaboration between artist and publisher. Some artists prefer to work with a particular writer or choose a specific text that holds special meaning, or one that is particularly compatible or provocative.

In each generation there are new translations or new attempts to bring to life classic legends, epic poems, and romances to which artists bring new dimensions of expression. Even in the apparently "straightforward instance of book illustration" in which "artists take off from pre-existing texts,"[5] one often finds that the artist's intention is not merely to provide graphic equivalents of textual matter. Inevitably, "the image maker, instead of groping for equivalents, will more likely seek within the text encouragement to provoke and transform rather than imitate and repeat" the substance and meaning of the text.[6]

The creation and production of a *livre d'artiste* is indisputably a labor of love. The artist, author, publisher, and printer must work together in varying degrees to achieve a high standard of workmanship and material. A successful project results only when the collaborators consider the interrelationships of design, text, image, typography, paper, printing, and binding. Such books are handmade, executed, and printed under the artist's supervision and published in limited editions. They employ original graphic techniques such as intaglio (etching, drypoint, aquatint, engraving, mezzotint), lithography, serigraphy, relief (woodcut and linocut), and photography. Because some of the preliminary and intermediate processes of production shed light on the complex evolution and the variety of techniques required to produce such works, this exhibition includes samples of preliminary drawings, maquettes, trial proofs, copperplates, *pochoirs* (stencils for handcoloring), special bindings, and other materials which relate to completed editions.

A consideration of the history of the *livre d'artiste* should begin with the late nineteenth century. From that time and well into the 1960s, in a period of extraordinary creative activity among artists, printers, and publishers, the production of *livres de peintres* flourished in France. Among the French artists who contributed to the genre were Redon, Bonnard, Rodin, Dufy, Braque, Rouault, Matisse, Picasso, Chagall, and Miró. Ambroise Vollard was, perhaps, the greatest of the French publishers of such books. Toward the end of the nineteenth century, he began to provide French artists with the patronage and commissions[7] that allowed them to pursue their interests in the inherently creative possibilities of book production. Vollard's support of the artists, his willingness to fund productions of the highest quality, and his ability to market the concept of the *livre de peintre* as a collector's item led to the extraordinary flowering of the genre in France.[8] His publication, in 1900, of Verlaine's *Parallèlment* with lithographs by Bonnard set the standard by which all other books of this genre have since been measured. Printed in pale rose, the illustrations spill over into the margins and areas normally reserved for text, and fully integrate in design and spirit with Verlaine's verse, creating one of the most beautiful volumes of this century. Between 1900 and 1939, Vollard published twenty-seven volumes (some of the most sumptuous of this century), in many cases leaving to each artist the choice of work to be illustrated.[9]

Other patrons and publishers of such books in this period included Daniel-Henry Kahnweiler, Albert Skira, Tériade (Efstratios Eleftheriades), and Iliazd (Ilia Zdanevitch), each of whom had an impact on the development of the modern artist-illustrated book.[10] In addition to the individual characteristics and interests which eventually defined each publisher's corpus of publications (as seen in the span of an entire career), these men shared the attributes of compelling vision, keen aesthetic judgment, and guiding presence[11] that enabled them to foster collaborations between artists, writers, and technicians, and to endure the vagaries of their time-consuming and expensive productions.

There was no such comparable explosion of interest in the *livre d'artiste*, among artists or publishers, in the United States during the period of its early flourishing in France. Significant numbers of American contributions to the genre have occurred only in the past three decades. In 1936, when Monroe Wheeler organized his seminal exhibition, *Modern Painters and Sculptors as Illustrators*, at the Museum of Modern Art in New York, he lamented:

> Where art is concerned, we Americans are a timid and ideal people. . . . Feeling a natural patriotism I wished to make the showing of American material as large as I could. But I found scarcely anything that one would patriotically choose to have compared with the best foreign work. With either quality or quantity in mind, one might suppose, if one did not know better, that this were a nation of extremely low cultural level, in a period of extreme poverty. . . . Our publishers and bibliophiles still prefer to play safe by entrusting craftsmen.[12]

When the Boston Museum of Fine Arts mounted its landmark exhibition, *The Artist & The Book: 1860–1960* (1961), Philip Hofer commented, "The United States, despite its size and wealth, is represented by scarcely one-quarter as many books as France."[13] As Hofer was writing these words in the 1960s, American artists began to show interest in the book as a medium for their works. Due to the passionate dedication and leadership of Tatyana Grosman, founder and director of Universal Limited Art Editions (ULAE),

American artists began to invent new and original approaches to the book. According to Lucien Goldschmidt, a great print connoisseur, "Hers was the first distinctly American contribution to modern art in making books."[14] Although the tradition of the *livre d'artiste* has been, historically, better appreciated in Europe and especially France since the turn of the century, the most adventurous and beautiful collaborations of the 1980s have originated in the United States. Among the books included here are several sponsored by the Library Fellows of the Whitney Museum of American Art's innovative program of fine-press publishing which began in 1982. Their Artists and Writers Series, the only museum-sponsored program of its kind, has produced a number of works that attest to the strength of the genre in the United States. In fact, this exhibition traces the apparent decline of European interest in artists' books and the simultaneous increase in American artists' activities in the genre.[15]

The decrease in interest and activity in Europe seems to have been related to several factors. Since 1973, most of the principal postwar European publishers (Editions Brunidor, Iliazd, Guy Lévis Mano [GLM], Tériade, Aimé Maeght) have died without passing on their dominance to younger publishers. In addition, the artists of the preceding four decades (Picasso, Ernst, Miró, Chagall, Dubuffet) who had created artists' books have also died. Paris has ceased to be the center of such publishing activity; important French editors of the 1980s are located in other regions of France—in Tarn, Montpellier, Vaucluse, and Losne. In the place of wealthy, visionary art dealers like Vollard and Kahnweiler, today's publishers of *livres d'artiste* are master fine art printers.

The history of book production has been a long one, originating centuries ago with the earliest form of book (and perhaps mankind's most durable art form), the codex—a quire of manuscript pages held together by stitching—which replaced the even earlier forms of written communication, wax tablets and scrolls. From the earliest period of its existence, the book had a coherent sequence of numbered pages and offered a spatial and temporal experience of cogent messages in a portable three-dimensional format. In our own century, and especially since the 1960s, the codex form has evolved, as *livre d'artiste*, in an expansive interpretation of its original form. The traditional book has been transformed into accordion, fan, scroll, and boxed format. Each page may present a point of view, contributing to an overall rhythmic flow, in a manner quite different from that of the consistent illustrational style of the traditional book.

The bindings of illustrated books have also evolved as contemporary artists have become intrigued with the inherent possibilities that binding presents. Bindings have long interested collectors and historians of all kinds of books but—even in the craft's most opulent and artistic manifestations of the medieval and renaissance periods—it was a skill practiced by artisans or craftsmen rather than artists. Bookbinders have always been specialists; but it is the artists of the twentieth century who have given the binding of the contemporary illustrated book the status of artistic expression, finding ways to adapt the requirements of bindings to their own particular expressive modes.

Artists' creativity and printers' ingenious techniques have kept pace with all that twentieth-century technology can offer to the art of book production. In the 1960s, there was a radical change in printmaking. Artists stopped being concerned with the chemistry of 'fine' printmaking and became interested in the final image, causing a new collaborative arrangement to develop between painters, sculptors, and craftsmen. New media, photographic aids, mass production, and a diversity of materials (including aluminum, canvas, rubber, mylar, vinyl, and other plastics) advanced a tendency toward three-dimensional work introduced through collage, assemblage, die-cutting, and the use of molds, and gave rise to the multiple object. There was a cross-over of ideas: methods used in graphic editions came to be used in the creation of illustrated books. More recently, renewed interest in papermaking, typesetting, bookbinding, and other book-related crafts, coupled with the involvement of contemporary artists in personal verbal and visual communication, has infused the illustrated book with new vitality.

The arts of the book offer an infinite variety of delights to the eye and intellect. This exhibition provides a rare opportunity to see 'great' books, illustrated by modern masters, removed from locked museum, library, and collectors' cabinets, and presented in the expansive manner they deserve. Often lavish and iconoclastic, these volumes invite an intimacy with each artist that cannot be acquired from a unique painting, drawing, or sculpture. These books will never become merely decorative, like art objects that hang on walls. They must be experienced at close range; their substance must be studied over a period of time to be understood. Reading is a slow, linear, and personal activity—quite different from other aspects of our popular culture. Preserved in their bindings, slip-cases, or boxes, relatively small in scale, formerly known only to those who sought them out, these books furnish in microcosm a comprehensive view of the art of the past twenty years.

Notes

[1] Philip Hofer, *The Artist & the Book: 1860–1960* (Boston: Museum of Fine Arts, 1961), p. 7.

[2] Ibid.

[3] Ibid., p. 8.

[4] Ibid.

[5] Roger Cardinal, "Comments and collaborations," review of *Surrealism and the Book*, by Renée Riese Hubert, *Times Literary Supplement*, 29 September–5 October 1989, p. 1064.

[6] Roger Cardinal, in the above-cited review, quotes directly from *Surrealism and the Book* (Berkeley: University of California Press, 1989).

[7] Hofer, p. 8.

[8] Ibid.

[9] Audrey Isselbacher, *Iliazd and the Illustrated Book* (New York: Museum of Modern Art, 1987), p. 13.

[10] For a detailed discussion, see the above-cited work, pp. 13–15.

[11] Isselbacher, p. 15.

[12] Monroe Wheeler, *Modern Painters and Sculptors as Illustrators* (New York: Museum of Modern Art, 1936), p. 22.

[13] Hofer, p. 9.

[14] Lucien Goldschmidt, *Print Quarterly* III, 3 (September 1986), p. 241.

[15] Antoine Coron, *Print Collector's Newsletter* XVII, 4 (September-October 1986), pp. 131–133.

POL BURY
Belgian, born 1922

Piccola guida all' uso di un viaggiatore in Italia
  by Maurice Stendhal
Milan, Sergio Tosi Stampatore, 1967
10 lithographs, 18½ × 14⅝ inches each page
Edition 130
Collection Loriano Bertini

■ In 1967, Belgian sculptor Pol Bury illustrated a new Italian translation of *Piccola guida all' uso di un viaggiatore in Italia* by French novelist and essayist Maurice Stendhal (Marie Henri Beyle; 1783–1842). The volume contains ten of Bury's lithographs picturing classic architectural and sculptural monuments. Bury, a kinetic sculptor, selectively cut circular patterns into photographic acetates before transferring images of famous sites, such as St. Peter's Basilica and the Colosseum in Rome, onto lithographic plates. Two black-and-white and eight four-color lithographs are printed off-register, suggesting the third dimension and the slow movement of Bury's kinetic sculptures. The unbound folio is presented in a wooden slipcase.

LUCIO FONTANA

Italian, 1899–1968

Portrait d' Antonin Artaud by Otto Hahn
Paris, Editions du Soleil Noir, 1968
Book and two of four multiples housed in painted
   wood box-sculpture
Book: 7¾ × 5¾ inches; each multiple: 7⅜ × 5 11/16 inches
   wood box-sculpture (closed): 14⅜ × 9⅜ × 2 9/16 inches
Edition 80
Collection The Museum of Modern Art, New York. Monroe
   Wheeler Fund.   932.69.

■ Otto Hahn's penetrating monograph, *Portrait d'Antonin Artaud* (1968) is not illustrated in a conventional sense. Lucio Fontana designed an ovoid free-standing object, lacquered in chartreuse. The sides of this multiple open perpendicular to the object; a line of holes riddles the center of each of the sides. One side of the object houses the leather-bound book. On the other side, various patterns slash and perforate four smaller oval-shaped die-cuts, each realized in a different material (steel, copper, opaque and transparent Plexiglas). Fontana's reduction to essential pictorial elements like lines and circles echoes Artaud's revolutionary idea of primordial theatre—innocent, uninhibited, and anti-realistic.

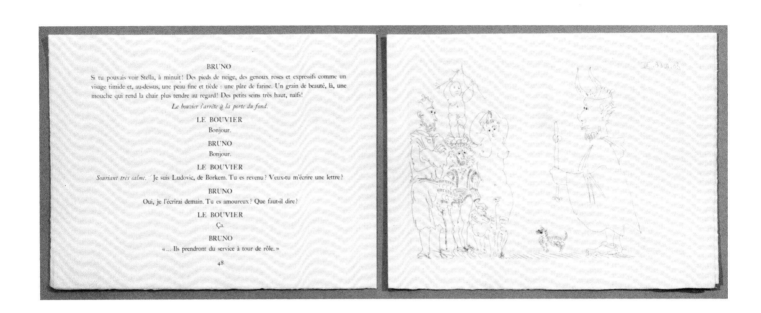

PABLO PICASSO

Spanish, 1881–1973

Le Cocu magnifique by Fernand Crommelynck
Paris, Atelier Crommelynck, 1968
7 etchings, 4 aquatints with etching, 1 aquatint with drypoint
    and etching, 11½ × 15 inches each page
Edition 200
Courtesy Irving Zucker Art Books, New York

■ Picasso illustrated 156 books during his lifetime. He knew Fernand Crommelynck and was inspired to illustrate his play, *Le Cocu magnifique*, which was first performed at the Théâtre de la Maison de l'Oeuvre in Paris in 1920 and published the following year. (Many years later Picasso met Crommelynck's sons, Aldo and Piero, who became his preferred master printers when they opened their atelier at Mougins in 1963. Atelier Crommelynck published *Le Cocu magnifique* in 1968.) Picasso executed the twelve intaglio prints for *Le Cocu*, four for each of the three acts, in late 1966. They allude to his personal mythology in which he associated the lascivious old minotaur with Bruno, the jealous husband of Stella, who because of his need to dominate the female soul is denied happiness and is eventually cuckolded. Picasso's full-page illustrations extend the meaning of the play; they are interspersed throughout the oblong folio which is covered by parchment wrappers and housed in a simple blood-red leather box. *Le Cocu* represents a continuation of the highest type of modern illustrated book and serves as a benchmark for the examples of the idiom that have appeared since 1968.

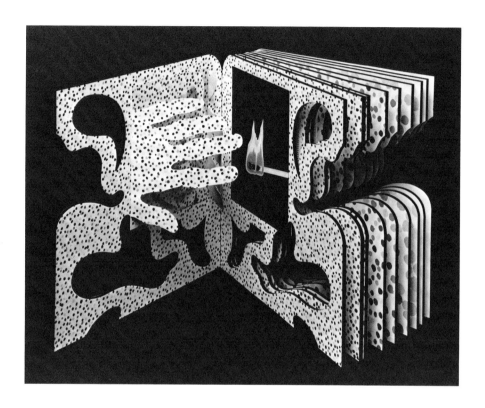

LUCAS SAMARAS
American, born Greece, 1936

Book by Lucas Samaras
New York, Pace Editions, 1968
11 color serigraphs with offset, embossing,
    thermography, die-cut, and collage mounted on masonite,
    10 × 10 inches each page
Edition 100
Courtesy Pace Editions, New York

■ Another unusual project published in 1968 is Lucas Samaras's *Book*. In this complex amalgam of texts and images, Samaras uses ninety-eight colors in five processes (screenprinting, offset lithography, embossing, thermography, and die-cutting) to construct an elaborate ten-page bound book.[1] *Book* is reminiscent, superficially, of indestructible children's books; the wild cut-out designs, paper foldouts (such as hands playing peek-a-boo), and miniature books tucked away in tiny pockets invite our participation in a fantasy world. But what initially appears to be innocent and enchanting turns sinister: Samaras's tales written to sound like nursery rhymes are scatalogical and menacing. The artist has composed every element to contribute to the reader's sense of anxiety and discomfort.

Rapunzel had long blond hair. When she heard the Enchantress calling she would wind it round a window-hook and let it down to the ground, so the old woman could climb up.

A few years later a Prince was riding through the forest and, as he passed by the tower, he heard a beautiful voice and stopped to listen: Rapunzel was singing. The Prince longed to see her and searched for a door but the tower had none. He couldn't forget her voice and came to listen every day. Then one afternoon he heard the Enchantress calling:

Rapunzel, Rapunzel
Let down your hair.

Rapunzel let down her hair and the Enchantress climbed up. 'Oh! If

DAVID HOCKNEY

British, born 1937

Six Fairy Tales from the Brothers Grimm
   translated by Heiner Bastian
Edition D
London, Petersburg Press, 1969
39 etchings, 17½ × 12⅛ inches each page
Edition 400
Courtesy Petersburg, London and New York

■ *Six Fairy Tales from the Brothers Grimm* (1969), illustrated by David Hockney and translated by Heiner Bastian from the original German edition by Manesse, consists of four separate editions.[2] Each volume includes thirty-nine etchings with closed-bolt pages, handsewn and bound. Each edition also contains a different set of six loose etchings in a sleeve, protected by a slipcase. Instead of using aquatints to achieve tone in the etchings, Hockney decided to emulate the technique of Giorgio Morandi in which the density of crosshatched line superbly creates various grays. Hockney's pictorial sources range from postcards and photographs from old German guidebooks to Leonardo da Vinci, Vittore Carpaccio, Paolo Uccello, Hieronymus Bosch, Pieter Bruegel, and René Magritte.

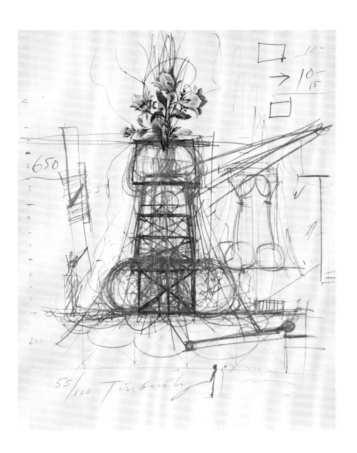

JEAN TINGUELY
Swiss, born 1925

La Vittoria
Milan, Sergio Tosi Stampatore, 1970
31 mixed-media prints, 19¼ × 13⅝ inches each page
Edition 100
Courtesy Sergio Tosi, Paris and Rome

■ *La Vittoria* (1970) is the title of the portfolio/book that documents Jean Tinguely's underground performance of a 'self-destructing' machine. The event took place on a Saturday evening in November, 1970. A crowd of about eight thousand people stood in the Piazza del Duomo in front of the Milan Cathedral where Tinguely's imposing sculpture had been erected and was hidden beneath purple drapery marked with the letters NR (*Nouveau Réalisme*) to commemorate the tenth anniversary of that movement. Tinguely had announced through the media that he was building a black machine which would turn into a white chariot that could be driven away. He assembled parts of the sculpture from various places in Milan, all the while keeping his real plans completely secret. On the evening of the event, the French poet and artist François Dufrêne mounted the rostrum and addressed the crowd in an animated unintelligible doublespeak of Italian-sounding words. Band music filled the square and, when the tension had risen to a fever pitch, the massive purple drapes fell forward revealing a gigantic phallus, about ten meters high, with testicles adorned with gold, plastic bananas and grapes. As the loudspeakers began to play "O Sole Mio," fireworks exploded from the sculpture.

Among the sixteen plates of the portfolio that commemorate the event are two aquatints, two lithographs, and one serigraph. The remaining eleven plates reproduce preliminary drawings and are handworked with pencil, ball-point pen, felt-tipped pen, pastels, watercolor, ink and decal, rubber stamps and feathers, and pen and ink stamps. Photographs, printed on tissue paper, document the actual event. A leather folder of the same color as the massive drapes that hid the phallus holds the loose sheets.

Ah! my heart, that's enough! Please!
Whenever I can't forget, you know,
My weaknesses break out in a sweat
Until, unclean, I let myself go.

Under my genius my heart curvets,
But, I tell you, just desperately!
If some young lady wants my life,
That's quite all right with me!

Oh go on, poor being, vehement soul!
Into their blasé Jordans, dive;
Just twice massaged with running life
And you'll be exorcized.

Who can answer me, alas?
You there, perhaps you know
What to do with a hypochondriac
Soul? Mine's really first-class.

O Helen, I roam my room;
And while you're down there having tea
In the wealth of some proud September day,
All of me shivers feverishly
Worrying about your health.

While, looking the other way . . .

PATRICK CAULFIELD

British, born 1936

Some Poems of Jules Laforgue
London, Petersburg Press, 1973
22 silkscreens, 16 × 14 inches each page
Edition 500
Collection Diane and Martin Ackerman

■ *Some Poems of Jules Laforgue* (1973) consists of twelve of the nineteenth-century French symbolist's poems illustrated by British artist Patrick Caulfield.[3] Between 1969 and 1972, Caulfield prepared twenty-two full-scale gouache studies for this project. There is a tangential relationship between the content of the poems and plates. Although figurative, the enlarged scale and reductive simplification of Caulfield's mundane subjects (which depict details of modern life, such as metal gates and railings, lamps, and windows) appear almost abstract. Uniform areas of flat color, outlined in black, refer to the style of children's coloring books. Unusual thick Neobond synthetic paper provides a perfect technical support for the screenprint medium.

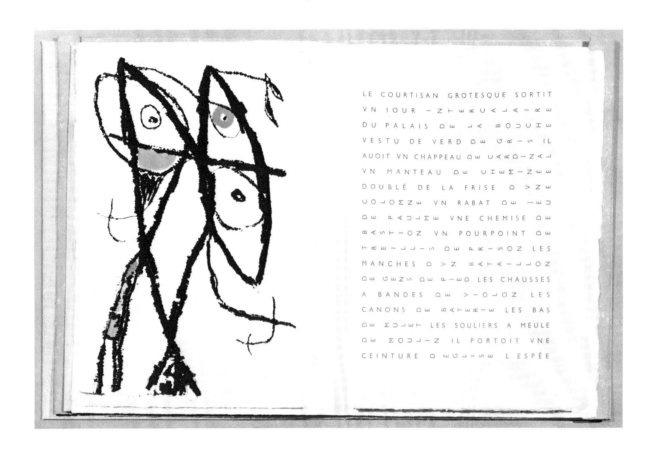

JOAN MIRÓ
Spanish, 1893–1983

Le Courtisan grotesque by Adrian de Monluc
Paris, Le Degré Quarante et Un, 1974
15 etchings with aquatint, 16½ × 11½ inches each page
Cover, 1 drypoint with aquatint, 16½ × 12⅜ inches
Edition 95
Courtesy Irving Zucker Art Books, New York

■ Iliazd, the Russian-born avant-garde poet, designer, and publisher, collaborated for twenty years with Joan Miró on *Le Courtisan grotesque* (1974), a seventeenth-century satire by Adrian de Monluc about an unattractive courtier. As with all the books he published, Iliazd exerted total control over the selection of the text and all aspects of design and production. The tale is reprinted from a unique 1630 edition in which certain words were italicized. The format appealed to Iliazd—with his strong interest in experimenting with language and typography—and he dissected de Monluc's text, organizing words without punctuation to parallel the double meanings imposed by typographical variations in the original edition. Each page differs because of the direction and spatial requirements of the letters. While much of the text proceeds normally from left to right, Iliazd printed the letters of the italicized words horizontally, thus demanding that the reader change his or her orientation and thought-process while reading the book. *Le Courtisan grotesque* is perhaps the finest example of Iliazd's extraordinary typographical transcriptions; it was the last of twenty *livres de peintres* that he issued in the period from 1940 to 1974. Like Picasso's *Le Cocu magnifique*, *Le Courtisan grotesque* represents a continuation of the highest type of work in the tradition of the *livre d'artiste*.

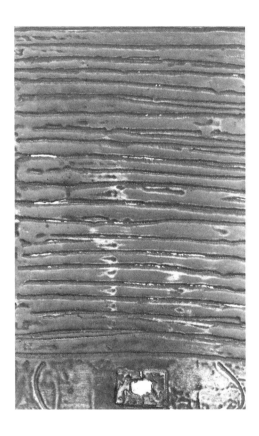 

ANTONI TÀPIES
Spanish, born 1923

Çà suit son cours by Edmond Jabès
Paris, Editions Fata Morgana, 1975
4 color etchings, 10¾ × 6¾ inches each page
Cover, inkless intaglio and etching, 10¾ × 6¾ inches
Edition 102
Courtesy Fundació Antoni Tàpies, Barcelona

■ Antoni Tàpies illustrated three books of poetry in 1975, including *Çà suit son cours* by Edmond Jabès. This traditionally-designed volume is elegant and beautifully produced. The cover is an inkless intaglio print randomly embossed with words over which the title is etched in brown. In addition, there are four abstract color etchings, one double-page and one in deep relief. Tàpies successfully fractures syntax, symbolically deconstructing the internal structure of words in the title while improvising with familiar geometric shapes such as the Greek cross. A special suite edition was printed on sheets with full margins, since the illustrations in the book are trimmed inside the plate-marks.

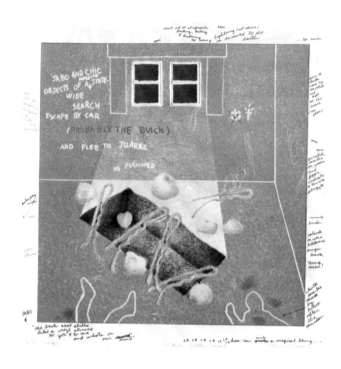

TERRY ALLEN

American, born 1943

Juarez
Chicago, Landfall Press, 1976
6 lithographs, 13¼ × 13¼ inches each page
33 rpm record
Edition 50
Courtesy Landfall Press, Chicago and New York

■ Until recently, Terry Allen's humorous art and music have drawn on a regional sensibility derived from his childhood in Lubbock, Texas.

Between 1969 and 1976, Allen created *Juarez* (1976), a three-part, autobiographical folk 'ballad' consisting of songs, prints, drawings, and assemblages, which tells the story of a quixotic journey through the southwest. *Juarez*, a boxed suite of six lithographs and a record album of songs, written and sung by the artist, is the final metamorphosis of the theme. Allen defines the characters—Jabo, a Juarez-born pachuco living in Los Angeles; Chic (Blundie), Jabo's girlfriend; Sailor, on leave in San Diego after a tour of duty in the Pacific; and Alice, a Tijuana prostitute—in terms of objects and places, all of which are interchangeable. "I

never thought of the characters as physical people . . . I always considered them to be atmospheres," reports Allen. "There are no people in the actual drawings . . . just allusions, hints, debris, after-the-facts and prior to, i.e., characters of the what-happened, the what-will and the inbetweens."[4] Marginal writing, inscribed around and within the lithographs (identifying characters, outlining and explaining details of the story), intimately connects relevant texts with the illustrations. The song lyrics printed on the back of the record album further amplify Allen's bizarre tale of love, passion, sexuality, and death.

R. BUCKMINSTER FULLER

American, 1895–1983

Tetrascroll by R. Buckminster Fuller
West Islip, New York, Universal Limited Art Editions, 1976
21 color lithographs, 30 11/16 × 35 3/8 inches each page
Edition 34
Collection Nancy and Edwin Marks

■ R. Buckminster Fuller's *Tetrascroll* (1976) is an extraordinary work that has a theoretical basis for text and illustrations. This cosmic fairy tale had its beginnings in 1930 when the scientist, inventor, designer, and thinker recounted *Goldilocks and the Three Bears* to his three-year-old daughter, Allegra. Instead of telling the traditional story, Fuller altered the text to explore his scientific interests. He made the bears into students who asked pertinent questions and got answers and explanations from Goldilocks, their teacher. In 1975, as an eightieth birthday present, artist-mathematician Edwin Schlossberg arranged for Fuller to meet Tatyana Grosman. The resulting book-object, *Tetrascroll*, can assume various sculptural configurations; it encapsulates fifty years of Fuller's thought. Twenty-six pages, each a thirty-six-inch equilateral triangle (one of the four faces of the tetrahedron, which Fuller established as the basic unit in nature) are bound as a book, opening to a length of approximately forty feet. Twenty-one lithographs relate to the text. The frameless images are printed in the same color and on the same page as the letterpress. Charming drawings decipher the intellectual and poetic meaning of the narrative.

GOTTFRIED HONEGGER
Swiss, born 1917

Zitat by Max Frisch
Zurich, Verlag 3, 1976
7 woodcuts, 8⅝ × 7¹⁄₁₆ inches each page
Edition 100
Courtesy Verlag 3, Zurich

■ In *Zitat* (1976), seven woodcuts by Swiss painter and sculptor Gottfried Honegger illustrate an ominous *poème concret* by Max Frisch. Abstract geometric woodcuts printed in black and red effectively use the wood grain to show texture, imply space, and provide visual animation. Honegger's emphasis on modesty, exactness, and harmony exemplifies the minimalist aesthetic and is comparable to Frisch's single-sentence poem: "A small population sees itself in danger: one has called a work force and people are coming."

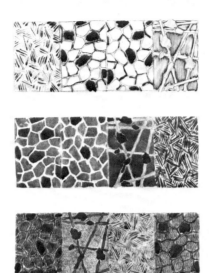

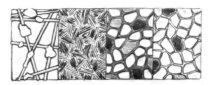

I gave up before birth,
it is not possible otherwise, but birth there had to be, it was he, I was inside, that's how I see it, it was he who wailed, he who saw the light, I didn't wail, I didn't see the light, it's impossible I should have a voice, impossible I should have thoughts, and I speak and think, I do the impossible, it is not possible otherwise, it was he who had a life, I didn't have a life, a life not worth having, because of me, he'll do himself to death, because of me, I'll tell the tale, the tale of his death, the end of his life and his death, his death alone would not be enough, not enough for me, if he rattles it's he who will rattle, I won't rattle, he who will die, I won't die, perhaps they will bury him, if they find him, I'll be inside, he'll rot, I won't rot, there will be nothing of him left but bones, I'll be inside, nothing left but dust, I'll be inside, it is not possible otherwise, that's how I see it, the end of his life and his death, how he will go about it, go about coming to an end, it's impossible I should know, I'll know, step by step, impossible I should tell, I'll tell, in the present, there will be no more talk of me, only of him, of the end of his life and his death, of his burial if they find him, that will be the end, I won't go on about worms, about bones and dust, no one cares about them, unless I'm bored in his dust, that would surprise me, as stiff as I was in his flesh, here long silence, perhaps he'll drown, he always wanted to drown, he didn't want them to find him, he can't want now any more, but he used to want to drown, he usen't to want them to find him, deep water and a millstone, urge spent like all the others, but why one day to the left, to the left and not elsewhither, here long silence, there will be no more I, he'll never say I any more, he'll never say anything any more, he won't talk to anyone, no one will talk to him, he won't talk to himself, he won't think any more, he'll go on, I'll be inside, he'll come to a place and drop, why there and not elsewhere, drop and sleep, badly because of me, he'll get up and go on, badly because of me, he can't stay still any more, because of me, he can't go on any more, because of me, there's nothing left in his head, I'll feed it all it needs.

JASPER JOHNS
American, born 1930

Foirades/Fizzles by Samuel Beckett
London and New York, Petersburg Press, 1976
33 etchings, 13⅛ × 9¹⁵⁄₁₆ inches each page
Cover, 1 serigraph, and 1 lithograph, 13⅛ × 9¹⁵⁄₁₆ inches
Edition 250
Courtesy Petersburg, London and New York

■ *Foirades/Fizzles* (1976) consists of five prose poems by writer Samuel Beckett and thirty-three etchings by painter Jasper Johns. This is an unusually beautiful collaboration—one in which words and images truly enhance each other. Vera Lindsay, an advisor to Petersburg Press, conceived of the writer-artist pairing and made the initial contacts. Johns and Beckett met in 1973. Beckett proposed collaborating on an early version of *Waiting for Godot*, but Johns would only consider illustrating new or unpublished material.

Beckett's dark essays, originally written in French between 1960 and 1972 (two were published in the French periodical *Le Minuit* in 1972–73) and rewritten in English by Beckett in 1974 for this project, relate to each other in subject, mood, and style, and elaborate upon his central themes: making sense of the void in man's search for self and the journey through birth, life, and death. Johns, assisted by Mark Lancaster, designed the book and arranged the sequence of the essays. Because Beckett had actually *rewritten* the essays in English rather than providing a strict translation, Johns decided to include both French and English versions (they were short and did not duplicate each other). United by a strange inner affinity, the plates do not illustrate Beckett's text per se. Based on *Untitled*, a large four-panel painting from 1972, all the etchings were executed in 1975 at the Atelier Crommelynck in Paris. Johns's elaborate variations on the themes of *Untitled*—stripes, rocks, body fragments—dissect and explore the permutations of each image. He questions the meaning of art by examining the gap between perception and creation. Johns admitted, "I like to repeat an image in another medium to observe the play between the two: the image and the medium."[5]

Although Beckett and Johns conceived the words and images of the book independently, Beckett's striking word 'pictures' inspired Johns, who was able to adapt his motifs by minimizing or elaborating details. *Foirades/Fizzles* is a virtual compendium of intaglio printmaking techniques; Johns uses etching, aquatint, soft-ground etching, sugar-lift, and photo etching, often combining the processes in a single print. Each of the five sections of the book opens with a full-page number or 'figure'. They are the only etchings in *Foirades/Fizzles* not related to *Untitled*. Double-page etchings separate the French and English versions of the text. The frontispiece and endpage are the book's only color etchings; they repeat crosshatching and flagstone designs from *Untitled* in the same three colors as the painting. This exceptional book is contained in a linen box (lined with lithographs that repeat the tricolor endpapers) designed for viewing as well as storage.

HANGIN UP *the frame.. to hang in there... is all yer doin anyway... (if the Vaqvoidues hung up the frame so can you) Even if theres sense to dwell on btwen... that spring and this fall I wout... step outside the frame to mention about playing at the edge of the garden the smoothe observer imagines this an that.. being observed.. Roughly speaking norm is lloyd. Do what you want.. to know this and that. Make threats for sure. Some would say that Pablo teased himself to death. I have thought as often.. death.. sure.. and why not.. with moments dropping like flys and dead leaves all around you— And tho you know some how it's so— or true— it's hard to point at or find a decent example when you want one.. Perhaps thatll do or this...*

WILLIAM T. WILEY

American, born 1937

Suite of Daze by William T. Wiley

Chicago, Landfall Press Inc., 1976

13 color intaglio prints, 16⅜ × 12⁹⁄₁₆ inches each page

Edition 50

Courtesy Landfall Press, Chicago and New York

■ Another original fable written and illustrated by an artist is William Wiley's *Suite of Daze* (1976). Wiley's alter ego, here called "Mr Unatural," chooses companions—Rembrandt Van Rijn, whom he calls Rim Rat, and Georges Seurat, dubbed Sir Rot—for the comic-like adventure and to track the Zen moment. "Before beginning the image plates," Wiley explains in the epilogue, "I would throw the coins for the I Ching—which has been a strong guide and source . . . I would consult the oracle [and] then begin a plate attempting to keep in mind the attitude suggested by the text. . . . The images for the plates occurred as I followed the clues of the dilemma's muse— Rim Rat on the trail of Sir Rot down the line and in the suds." Among the thirteen whimsical etchings are four hexagrams (*Obstruction*, *Innocence [The Unexpected]*, *The Well*, and *Progress*) and their interpretations which blend with the tale. Wiley reveals his humor through the layered combinations and juxtapositions of words and images. In *Glittering Remains*, the last etching in the book, Wiley depicts the void that contradicts and embraces form, in this case the shadow of Rim Rat.[6]

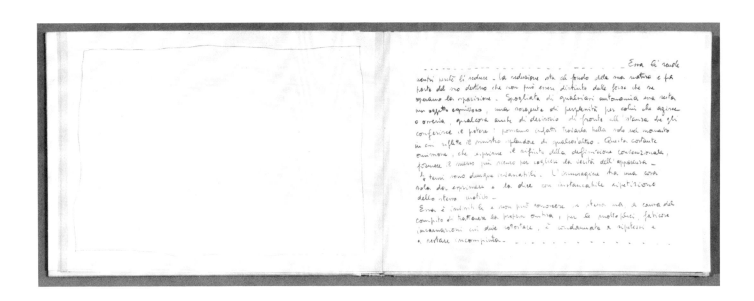

MARCO GASTINI

Italian, born 1938

Pantomima by Ugo Leonzio
Genoa, Franco Mello & Giorgio Persano Editori, 1977
21 lithographs and serigraphs,
 13⅞ × 19¾ inches each page
Edition 40
Collection Loriano Bertini

■ In *Pantomima* (1977), twenty-one lithographs and serigraphs by Marco Gastini are assembled in five large, oblong folios with accordion-bound pages that fold out in all directions. Text selections from *Norma*, by Ugo Leonzio,[7] are printed in script as well as block letters over and adjacent to the graphics. Pictures dominate the decorative text with no discernable descriptive interpretation of the author's ideas. Each section slowly reveals its perspective. The book opens with a white print edged in black. It ends with "Pantomima" in mirror-writing on a black background. As pages unfold, the use of minimal black and red rectangles, delicate lines, some printed in the colors of the rainbow, reverberate, forcing comparisons between different prints.

GIULIO PAOLINI

Italian, born 1940

Sei illustrazioni per gli scritti sull'Arte Antica di Johann J. Winckelmann

Genoa, Franco Mello & Giorgio Persano Editori, 1977

6 serigraphs and lithographs,

  17 × 13⅜ inches each page

Edition 40

Collection Loriano Bertini

■ *Sei illustrazioni per gli scritti sull' Arte Antica di Johann J. Winckelmann* (1977) is a large, elegant, bound volume that reproduces six Winckelmann essays with graphics by postmodernist Italian artist Giulio Paolini. The teachings of Winckelmann (1717–68), first of the great German art historians, founder of Neo-Classicism and champion of "the noble simplicity and calm grandeur of Greek art" had a profound influence on late-eighteenth and early-nineteenth-century painters.

Paolini, grounded in the ideas of the Renaissance and Mannerism, uses photography (transformed here through serigraphy and lithography) "to produce a simulacrum." For Paolini, "a photograph is a skin, an intangible diaphragm which provides this miracle of representation."[8] In this volume, the artist explores the relation of art to history and theory.

LARRY RIVERS
American, born 1923

The Donkey and the Darling by Terry Southern
West Islip, New York, Universal Limited Art Editions, 1977
52 color lithographs, 18½ × 21½ inches each page
Edition 35
Courtesy Rose Art Museum, Brandeis University,
   Waltham, Massachusetts   Anonymous Gift

■ When Tatyana Grosman approached Larry Rivers about illustrating a second book for ULAE (he had already completed the remarkable *Stones* (1957-59) with Frank O'Hara), he asked his friend Terry Southern to supply a text. *The Donkey and the Darling* (1977), a fanciful adult parable, is the product of their collaboration. Southern's morality tale takes place in Sillicreechie, where the young heroine, Darling, lives. Donkey, a proud fool who constantly gets into trouble, is in reality a large black woolly dog. Bad Witch, disguised as a hypodermic needle, owns a copy of every printed book in existence, and devours their contents to find secret information to plague Darling and her other victims.

A forest-green lacquered wooden box con-

tains fifty-two lithographic pages. Rivers designed the cover, a green free-form, hand-blown glass inset (alluding to the swill hole of the story) through which one reads the artist's and author's names and the book title, printed on a mirror. Rivers has color-coded each of the satire's eighteen characters so that each character's name always appears in the same shade throughout the text. All the main characters return for a 'curtain call' on the last page. The artist and author chose an eccentric gothic typeface for the text and, like Iliazd, freely compose the structure of every line of type to emphasize meaning. The production of the book required 500 separate press runs of the 166 lithographic stones and 334 plates that the artist used.

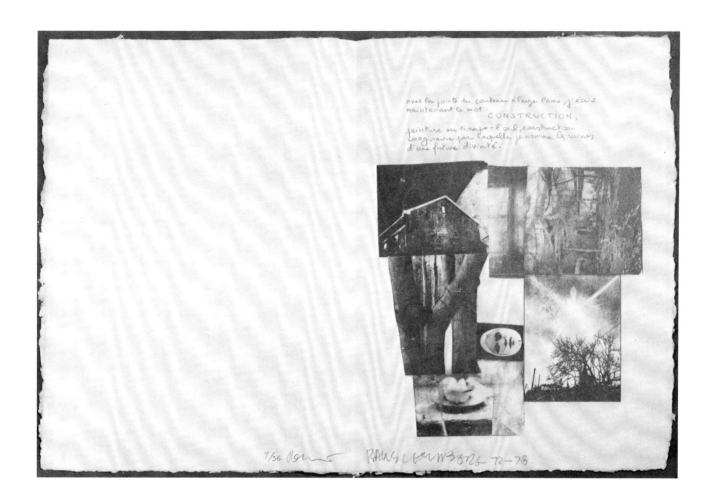

ROBERT RAUSCHENBERG

American, born 1925

Traces suspectes en surface by Alain Robbe-Grillet
West Islip, New York, Universal Limited Art Editions, 1978
36 color lithographs, 27 × 20 inches each page
Edition 36
Private collection

■ *Traces suspectes en surface* (1978) is the product of a collaboration between Alain Robbe-Grillet and Robert Rauschenberg.[9] The book's title is a pun on the term used by the French police for a suspicious situation and refers literally to Robbe-Grillet and Rauschenberg's marks on the twenty-seven lithographic plates and thirty-seven stones used in the production of the work.[10] There is no plot or narrative but, like the images, the prose poem presents oblique metaphors.

Rauschenberg chose the design, colors, and paper for the book. Through color placement, gradation, or variation, the three main color themes—red, gray, and ochre—unfold. Rauschenberg laid out the words of the text to complement his transfer images: some pages are completely covered with Robbe-Grillet's flawlessly handwritten French text; others have text at the top and bottom of a page with empty space between, and still others have text only in the top quadrant. Some pages are touched by the smallest gesture—a vertical blue-gray line, an ochre ground for the writing, the words in a spectrum of reds. Others are jammed with recognizable images transferred from European magazines. Occasionally, an image coincides exactly with the text—for example, eggs on a plate, or a bull—but, by mutual agreement, neither artist nor author wanted to illustrate the work of the other. On the first page of an elaborate four-page colophon, Rauschenberg summarized the collaboration in the following way: "Book is exchange with image and text." Contained in a simple fire-red clothbound box, *Traces suspectes en surface* combines technical economy with visual and material sumptuousness.

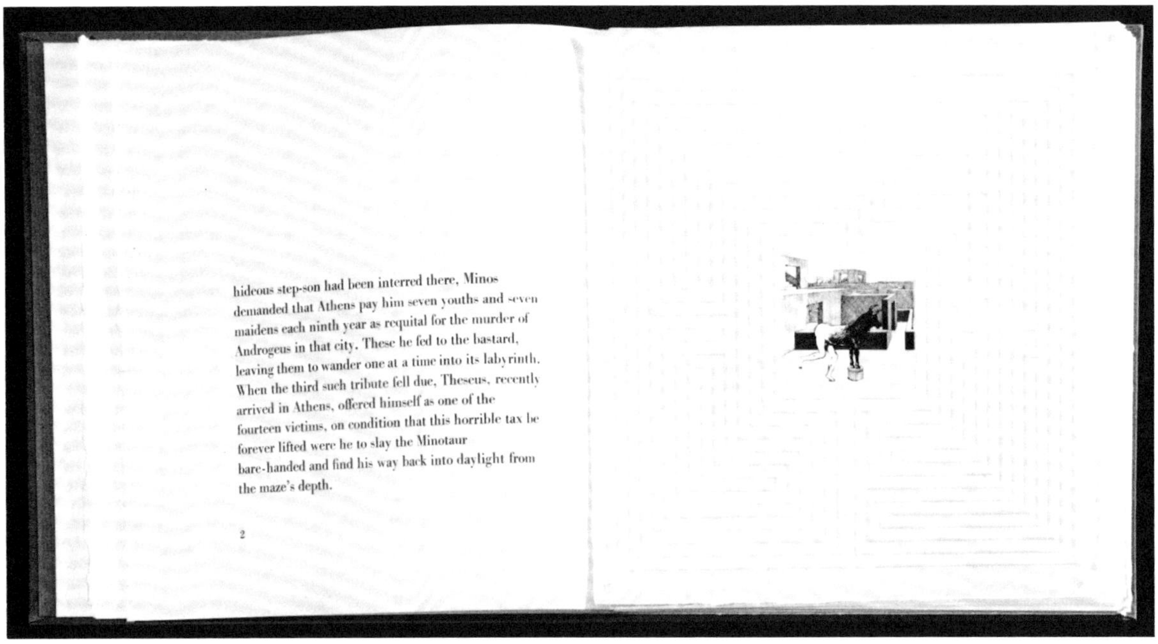
hideous step-son had been interred there, Minos
demanded that Athens pay him seven youths and seven
maidens each ninth year as requital for the murder of
Androgeus in that city. These he fed to the bastard,
leaving them to wander one at a time into its labyrinth.
When the third such tribute fell due, Theseus, recently
arrived in Athens, offered himself as one of the
fourteen victims, on condition that this horrible tax be
forever lifted were he to slay the Minotaur
bare-handed and find his way back into daylight from
the maze's depth.

2

JOHN FURNIVAL

British, born 1933

Blind Date by Thomas Meyer
Guildford, Circle Press, 1979
10 etchings and embossed prints including 1 color etching and aquatint, 11 × 11 inches each page
Edition 335
Collection Diane and Martin Ackerman

■ *Blind Date* (1979), with illustrations by John Furnival and text by Thomas Meyer, is a visual and verbal interweaving of two Greek myths that deal with strength and courage: Theseus' heroic slaying of the Minotaur and Hercules' punishment by Zeus and enslavement by Omphale. The myth of Minos and the Minotaur has inspired artists throughout history, including Matisse and Picasso in the twentieth century. Although there are stylistic differences and each interpretation is strikingly different, the various versions are faithful to the story. "Historical accuracy is not a problem," according to Furnival. "We hope that it is an essay in enjoyment, that is all."[11] Each of the ten small, accurately drawn and shrewdly detailed etchings is placed at the center of a different maze which has been blind-embossed on rag paper and inserted into unbound sections of the text.

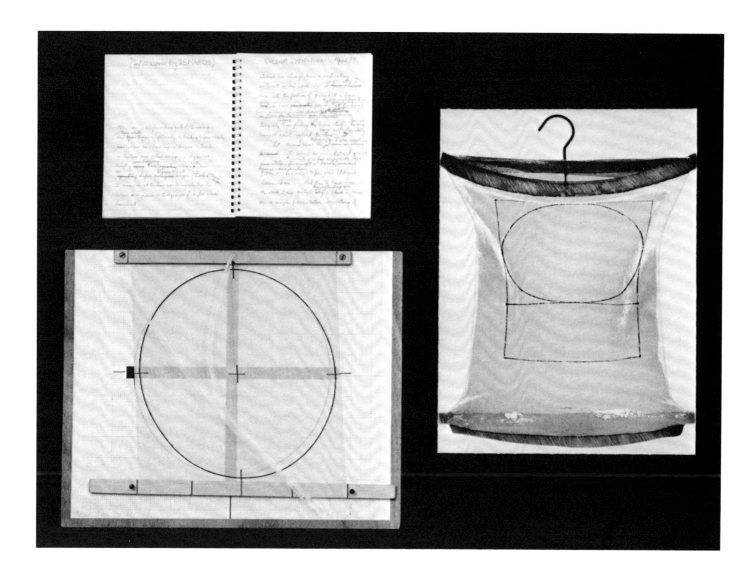

MICHAEL KIDNER
British, born 1917

The Elastic Membrane
Guildford, Circle Press, 1979
2 spiral-bound books: *Notebook*, 7⅛ × 6¾ inches;
   Continuity Book, 9¾ × 8¼ inches
6 prints: 3 photo etchings, 16¾ × 13 inches each page;
   3 continuous-tone lithographs, 16½ × 13 inches each page
Multiple object, 17 × 13¼ × ⅞ inches
Malaysian plywood box with Perspex cover,
   17⁷⁄₁₆ × 14 × 2½ inches
Edition 300
Collection Diane and Martin Ackerman

■ British artist Michael Kidner's *The Elastic Membrane* (1979) consists of an unconventional assemblage of three photo etchings and three continuous-tone lithographs; a model of an ingenious drawing machine which generates prints; and two offset spiral-bound notebooks that record the artist's intellectual journey using this device. One of the notebooks reproduces eight drawings and nine photo etchings as well as the constructions from which they were made. All are gathered in a wooden box protected by a Perspex slipcase. In an effort to de-mystify constructivist artistic intentions, the artist has chosen this transparent approach to explain process. "The use of elastic [in the drawing apparatus]," Kidner explains, "grew out of my dissatisfaction with stretching my wavy line grids first numerically and then with computers. The physicality of making my own 'Heath Robinson computer' results from my search to incorporate a living dimension (in the sense of the personal, the psychological and the organic) alongside, as it were, the rational forms I deal with in my work."[12]

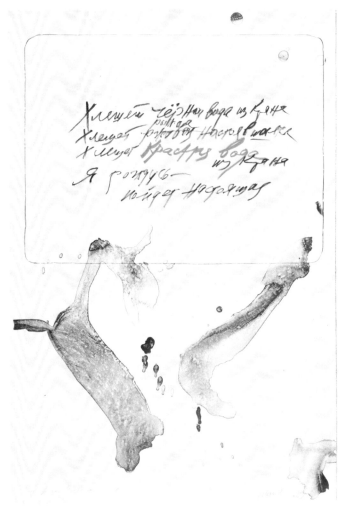

ALEXANDER LIBERMAN

American, born Russia, 1912

Nostalgia for the Present by Andrei Voznesensky
West Islip, New York, Universal Limited Art Editions, 1979
19 lithographs, 40¾ × 27⁵⁄₁₆ inches each page
Edition 28
Collection of the Grunwald Center for the Graphic Arts,
University of California, Los Angeles, Gift of the
Friends of the Graphic Arts and the UCLA Art Council
in honor of E. Maurice Bloch

■ *Nostalgia for the Present* (1979) is a collaboration that brings together the passionate poetry of Andrei Voznesensky and majestic lithographs by Alexander Liberman.[13] The artist and the poet made joint decisions about the format and design of the seventeen-page book: Voznesensky anticipated the size and shape; Liberman selected type, binding, and the sequential placement of images in relation to text. For three of ten stanzas in the poem, the artist incorporated his ideas with the poet's on a single page. For other stanzas, they used two sheets for text and image. The book's conceptual purity and starkness—printed in black and white—are interrupted only once in the ninth stanza, in which red is used as a symbol for blood. This is the only instance in which image is subservient to the menacing weight of the printed word.

Liberman used one large stone to produce the lithographic illustration for the last stanza. He drew all the other images on plates that contained remarkably beautiful tusche washes usually achieved only on stone surfaces. Voznesensky was immediately responsive to the idea of mirror writing on the stone: he wrote each stanza deliberately, crossing out mistakes and rewriting corrections above his original notations, with the effect of underscoring meaning. He insisted on printing the edges of the limestone slabs to show he had worked directly on stone. The strength of the drawing is a perfect match to the power of the word.

DOTTY ATTIE
American, born 1938

Mother's Kisses
New York, Solo Press Inc., 1982
26 handcolored images and words, 6 × 6 inches each page
1 lithograph, 35¾ × 26½ inches
Edition 32
Courtesy Solo Press Inc., New York

■ Dotty Attie combines mysterious and humorous text with 'borrowed' visual elements. *Mother's Kisses* (1982) is part of a series that reinterprets and deconstructs masterpieces from the history of art. Twenty-six small handcolored lithographs, alternating images and text, are individually framed in six-inch-square mats. Each illustration in the boxed series is a detail from a large handcolored, lithographic rendition of Agnolo Bronzino's *Venus, Cupid, Folly, and Time* (National Gallery, London). Like close-up stills from a film, a love story between mother and son unfolds. The narrative begins: "Mother and he had always been very close." The next frame shows the face of a beautiful young boy. "They did everything together." Pictures of a woman's breast held by a small hand, and a partial view of her head, follow. Innuendos continue: "Friends often commented on the touching relationship they shared." In a precise, realistic style reminiscent of Ingres, Attie translates the icy obscenity of Bronzino's mannerist canvas. She uses the book's sequential format to reveal personal attitudes and unexpected details about one of history's most famous artists and his masterwork.

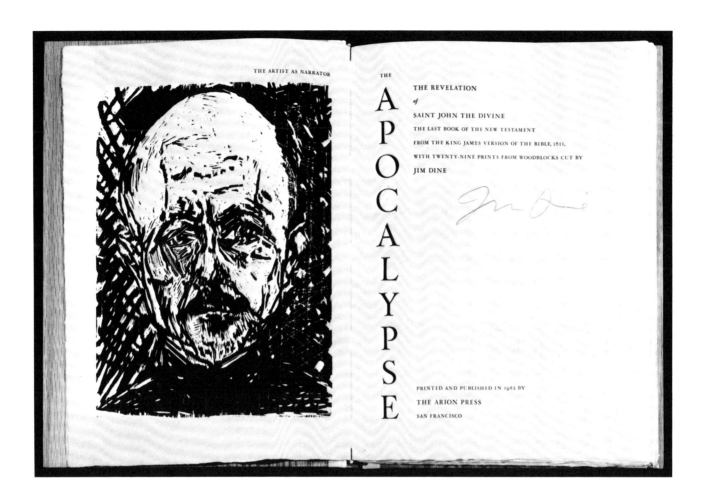

JIM DINE
American, born 1935

The Apocalypse: The Revelation of St. John the Divine
San Francisco, Arion Press, 1982
29 woodcuts, 15 × 11¼ inches each page
Edition 150
Courtesy of the artist

■ Jim Dine created twenty-nine woodcuts from oak blocks for an edition of *The Apocalypse: The Revelation of St. John the Divine* (1982), from the King James version of the Bible. Arion Press had suggested a number of subjects for Dine. Stirred by his reading of *Unforgettable Fire: Pictures Drawn by Atomic Bomb Survivors*,[14] Dine chose the turbulent last book of the New Testament, thereby associating his work with historic woodcut prototypes in traditional Bible illustration. Beginning with a self-portrait frontispiece entitled *The Artist as Narrator*, Dine employed many signature images, carefully selecting corresponding references in the text. Two robes relate to *Robes Were Given Unto Everyone* and *Arrayed in White Robes*; two entwined trees represent *My Two Witnesses Two Olive Trees*; tools refer to *Pruning Shears*; a broken heart is associated with *The Voice of the Bridegroom and the*

Bride; a skull illustrates *There Shall Be No More Death* and *Death and Hell Delivered up the Dead*.

Dine is one of the first artists in the contemporary period to re-explore the potentials of woodblock printing. Here, his conventional woodcuts paraphrase the strong contrasts in black and white that are reminiscent of the German woodcut tradition. In describing his process, Dine confessed, "I don't really cut them spontaneously. I make elaborate drawings and follow them exactly. I take a brush and use India ink and I draw on the wood and let it dry. I spend days and weeks sitting with the wood on my lap (or on sawhorses) using the Dremel, following it exactly. It's so soothing. It's like you put yourself into another state. You think about a lot of other things but you are also inventing as you go along."[15]

MARKUS LÜPERTZ
German, born 1941

Ich Stand vor der Mauer aus Glas by Markus Lüpertz
Berlin, Galerie Springer, 1982
10 color lithographs and 1 watercolor,
  16½ × 11 ¹⁵⁄₁₆ inches each page
Edition 220
Courtesy Galerie Springer, Berlin

■ Recently, more artists have begun to illuminate their own texts. In 1982, Markus Lüpertz's *Ich stand vor der Mauer aus Glas*, a volume of poetry and ten lithographs appeared in conjunction with the Neo-expressionist's painting exhibition in Berlin at Galerie Springer. Lüpertz's self-referential themes are well matched to his powerful red, yellow, and black pictures of heads and masks.[16]

MATTA

(Roberto Antonio Sebastian Matta Echaurren)
Chilean, born 1911

Ubu Roi by Alfred Jarry
Paris, Dupont-Visat, L'Inéditeur, 1982
8 handcolored engravings, 16⅛ × 10¼ inches each page
Edition 165
Courtesy L'Inéditeur, Paris (Christine and Albert Dupont)

■ *Ubu Roi* (1982), by Alfred Jarry, contains eight engraved plates by Matta (Roberto Antonio Sebastian Matta Echaurren), a second-generation surrealist who had been influenced by Jarry's work. Matta collaborated on this book with Parisian publisher-printer Dupont-Visat. He patterned his illustrations after Mayan carvings and comic strips, making sketches before executing the eight engraved plates which are hand-wiped in many colors, requiring enormous skill and attention in printing. For the engraved cover of the book, Albert Dupont developed a new procedure to produce the relief effect. The complete text is printed from a late-nineteenth-century first edition, using the original typography transformed by sketches, remarques, and calligrams. Dupont remembers, "We had fun playing day after day with new ideas."[17]

DANIEL BUREN
French, born 1938

D'une impression l'autre
Neuchâtel, Editions Media and the Artist, 1983
30 serigraphs and 30 color photographs,
 13⅛ × 20½ inches each page
Edition 95
Courtesy of the artist

■ In fifteen years of book making, artist Daniel Buren has always written his own texts. Initially he justified his 'literary' activity as a way to avoid misinterpretation of his work. Later the texts took on lives of their own, resulting from reflections, commissions, and the pure pleasure of writing. In *D'une impression l'autre* (1983), Buren pairs small souvenir photos with full sheets of screenprinted stripes. The snapshots record thirty manifestations/ exhibitions between 1970 and 1982; the stripes quote the same systemic configuration he has explored to transform space in public settings such as billboards, subway interiors, building facades, walls, and windows. "What is a photographic document worth that is supposed to reproduce a work that has disappeared?" asks Buren in the introduction. "Having captured and fixed a moment of reality, how does the photograph give it back to us? Is it reliable evidence?" These questions form the subject of the book. The width of the screenprinted stripes coincides with the artwork. Buren reproduces cibachrome photographs from negatives, some of which are fifteen years old and faded. Whites, for instance, are no longer pure and are transformed in the screenprints. Buren forces the viewer to compare one print with another and confront the paradox of a souvenir photo that fades like the memory it represents.

ALBERT DUPONT

French, born 1951

Nathalie et Justine
Paris, L'Inéditeur, 1983
Book/object, 5½ × 9 × 2¾ inches
Edition 24
Courtesy L'Inéditeur, Paris

■ Albert Dupont's *Nathalie et Justine* (1983) is an example of a sculptural book. Dupont, a lettrist artist interested in phonetic poetry, had always been fascinated by Stéphane Mallarmé's *Un Coup de des . . .* which transformed the conventional method of reading poetry because of its "radical typographical arrangement . . . and emphasis on the idea of chance."[18] When Dupont heard about Rubik's Cube from a friend, he conceived of a playful interpretation which would combine a lettrist poem (*lettrie* in French) and 'hypergraphic' images (signs). Because the puzzle delighted his daughters Nathalie and Justine, Dupont titled the book-object after them, subtitling it *"(lettrimage)³"* to suggest the infinite possibilities inherent in assembling both poem and images. Dupont played with colors, mixing tints on each face of the cube to increase visual richness. This super-temporal, ever-changing poem-painting encourages the viewer to explore the infinite options of interpretation intrinsic to the object.[19]

ROBERT MOTHERWELL
American, born 1915

El Negro by Rafael Alberti, translated by Vincente Lléo Cañal
Mount Kisco, New York, Tyler Graphics Ltd., 1983
19 lithographs, 15 × 15 inches; 15 × 25¾ inches;
  15 × 37¾ inches
Edition 51
Courtesy Tyler Graphics Ltd., Mount Kisco, New York

■ The nineteen lithographs that comprise *El Negro* (1983) are the product of an intense dialogue which began about 1967. At that time, Robert Motherwell chanced upon Rafael Alberti's *Selected Poems* in which small portions of Alberti's moving homage to the art of painting entitled *A la pintura* were published. Alberti's series of poems apparently stirred Motherwell's innermost feelings and became the subject of his magnificent first *livre d'artiste* published by ULAE in 1972. The two artists met in 1980 at the Madrid opening ceremonies of a retrospective of Motherwell's paintings. Alberti unexpectedly rose from his seat, moved toward the podium and, in an electrifying voice, read *El Negro Motherwell*, a poem he had written for the occasion. After their meeting, Motherwell decided to illuminate Alberti's poetic tribute.[20]

As in *A la pintura*, Motherwell took an untraditional approach to design. The pages of *El Negro* come in three sizes, the larger sheets opening out horizontally either once or twice. Occasional patches of color—ochre for the earth, blue for the sky and sea—interrupt the passionate, mysterious blacks that define bold, eloquent images which further explore the challenging themes of Motherwell's Spanish Elegy series. Motherwell extracts the titles for his lithographs from the sensuous words and vigorous lines of the poem: *Black wall of Spain, Through black emerge purified, Elegy black black*. A binding device which holds the pages together as a book has a detachable bar that permits the pages to be removed for exhibiton or custom binding. In *El Negro*, Motherwell and Alberti collaborated in the fullest sense of the word—each one creating for the other.

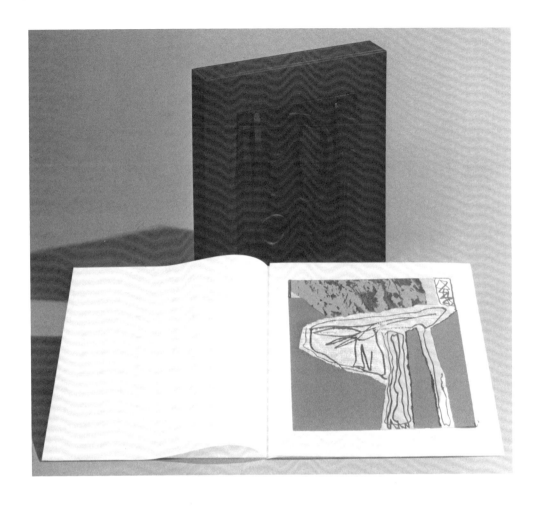

LOUISE NEVELSON

American, born Russia, 1900–1988

Nevelson's World by Jean Lipman
New York, Hudson Hills Press, Inc. and Pace Editions, 1983
1 seven-color serigraph, 13 × 12 inches
Black polyester-resin multiple on box cover,
  9⅝ × 8½ × ⁷⁄₁₆ inches
Edition 100
Courtesy Pace Editions, New York

■ The binding of *Nevelson's World* (1983), a monograph by Jean Lipman with an introduction by Hilton Kramer, harks back to her mysterious wall constructions. A black polyester resin multiple is bonded to the lid of a black clothbound portfolio. Nevelson also created a silkscreen print, in the style of her more recent metal tree sculptures, entitled *My World is in This Box* which was slipped into the volume.

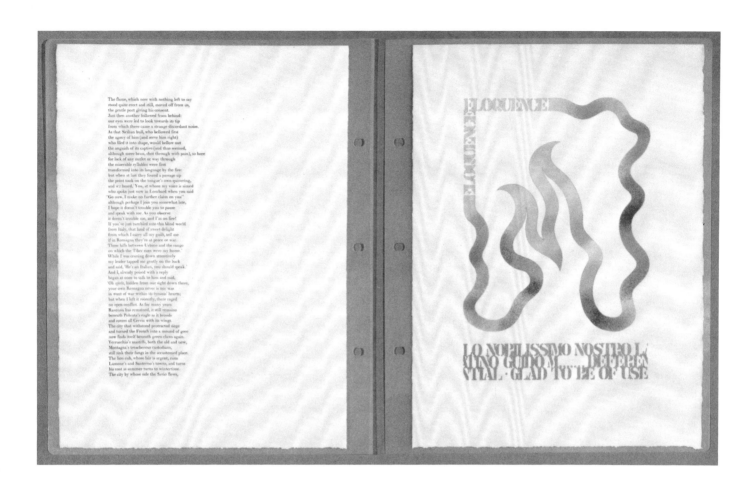

TOM PHILLIPS

British, born 1937

Inferno by Dante Alighieri

London, Talfourd Press, 1983

3 volumes

34 folios containing various combinations of etching,
lithograph, and serigraph, 16⅜ × 12½ inches each page

Edition 85

Collection Tom Phillips

■ The first book of Dante's *Divine Comedy* (ca. 1307–1321), *Inferno*, which describes hell and the suffering of the damned, has provided an irresistible challenge to artists—from early manuscript illuminators, to Sandro Botticelli, William Blake, and Robert Rauschenberg. British artist Tom Phillips's version (1983), in which he served as translator, artist, designer, and publisher, contributes a modern visual commentary to Dante's text.[21] "The range of imagery," explains the artist, "matches Dante's in breadth, encompassing everything from Greek mythology to the Berlin Wall, from scriptural reference to a scene in an abbatoir and from alchemical signs to lavatory graffiti. Similarly, the range of modes of expression is wide, including as it does early calligraphy, collage, golden-section drawings, maps, diagrams, doctored photographs, quotations from earlier works of art and specially programmed computer graphics."[22] Phillips employs the intaglio processes, lithography (stone, plate, and offset), screenprinting, and letterpress, individually and in combination, to realize the illustrations for his version of Dante. Embedded in the translation is a parallel text, a commentary on Dante from W. H. Mallock's *A Human Document*, a little-known Victorian novel that formed the basis of Phillips's earlier 'worked-on text', *A Humument*.

Each of thirty-four cantos is twelve pages long and contains a thematic frontispiece and three images.[23] Throughout the project, Phillips paid careful attention to Dante's preoccupation with magic numbers, such as three and nine. He uses both obvious and subtle visual information to explain Dante's writing and to establish structural continuity. The emblematic lily representing the city of Florence, for example, changes as the work progresses, showing Dante's fluctuating attitude toward his city.

Phillips worked on the Dante for seven years, collaborating with papermakers, typesetters, printers in several media, binders, bankers, collectors, museums, and galleries—all the while functioning creatively as an artist and translator. The inventiveness and care with which he resolved each aspect of the book's production is testimony to his commitment of time and energy. A portfolio of nine screenprints was published in conjunction with the book. For images like *Dante in his Study*, which has twenty-seven separate colors, a format larger than page size was required because of the technical complexity of the printing process.

WOLFGANG GAFGEN

German, born 1936

En Bas by Olivier Kaeppelin

Paris, Editions Baudoin Lebon, 1984

15 intaglios, 13¾ × 15¾ inches each page

Edition 90

Courtesy Galerie Baudoin Lebon, Paris

■ *En Bas* (1984) contains poetry by Olivier Kaeppelin and fifteen superb full-page intaglio illustrations by Wolfgang Gafgen. Gafgen builds his own complementary visual text, translating the photographic precision of his drawings into the intaglio technique, lettering some plates with cryptic messages that refer to the text. He confines images of tents, woodpiles, and fires within a circle which serves as a metaphor of the eternity of hell interpreted through man's endless cycle of building and destruction.

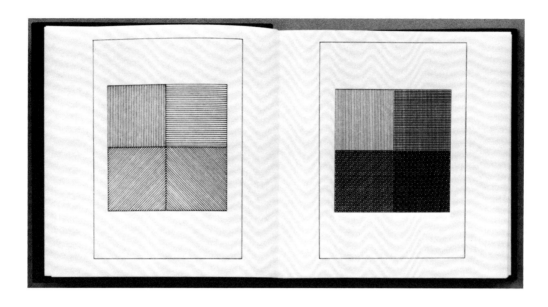

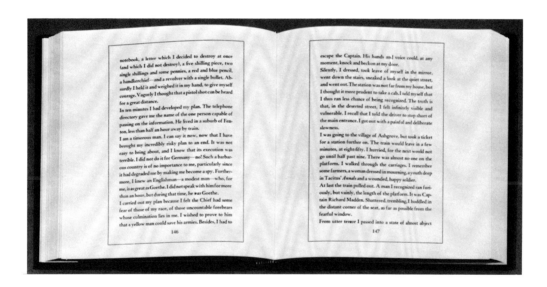

SOL LeWITT
American, born 1928

Ficciones by Jorge Luis Borges
New York, The Limited Editions Club, Ltd., 1984
22 serigraphs, 8 × 8 inches each page
Edition 1500
Courtesy The Limited Editions Club, Ltd., New York

■ *Ficciones* (1984), Jorge Luis Borges's collection of writings illustrated with twenty-two silkscreens after drawings by Sol LeWitt, is bound in simple black cowhide. The stark design of the book conveys the rigor of both the artist's and author's spare, formal vocabulary. A black rectangle frames each image or page of writing, and a print introduces each composition. A linear pattern provides a background screen for the artist's geometric figures which are defined by densities of hatched lines. LeWitt transforms shapes in serial progressions that parallel Borges's short, pungent fantasies and imaginings.

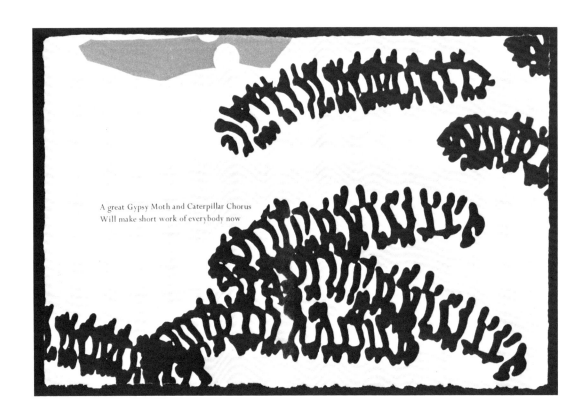

A great Gypsy Moth and Caterpillar Chorus
Will make short work of everybody now

JUDY RIFKA
American, born 1945

Opera of the Worms by Rene Ricard
New York, Solo Press Inc. and Joe Fawbush Editions, 1984
15 color lithographs, 12 × 9 inches each page
Edition 80
Courtesy Solo Press Inc., New York

■ Rene Ricard's frivolous love story, *Opera of the Worms* (1984), begins: "There's a song among the flowers in the evening." The anthropomorphized poem set in a garden tells the story of a lawn, the main character, who throws his grassy self at the feet of a prima donna rose. The grass is scorned and ultimately destroyed by gypsy moths and caterpillar villains. Judy Rifka's agitated black line drawings with bold patches of color discreetly follow textual references and are a pictorial complement to the Darwinian tale. The ten unbound folios contain fifteen double-page lithographs, as well as a lithograph on the cover of the paper wrappers.[24]

MARK BEARD

American, born 1956

The Côte d'Azur Triangle by Harry Kondoleon
New York, Vincent Fitz Gerald & Co., 1985
7 color lithographs, 11 etchings,
    14⅛ × 12⅛ inches each page
Edition 119
Courtesy Vincent Fitz Gerald & Co., New York

■ Playwright Harry Kondoleon and artist Mark Beard share an interest in classical Greek and Roman art and history. Beard provided illustrations for Kondoleon's play, *The Côte d'Azur Triangle* (1985), one part of a trilogy of plays written in Bali and patterned after classical tragedy. The illustrations relate directly to Kondoleon's cold and witty drama of the not-so-classic love triangle in which the third party is the husband's male lover. Beard employs classic details, such as a proscenium arch and caryatids, as part of the compositions, and combines lithography and etching. Kondoleon wanted to give the book a juvenile look and requested large type. Beard, who likes the unconventional, decided to use gatefolds, collage, and paper-doll cutouts. Eight printers proofed more than seventy plates over a period of seven months to realize this unusual book.

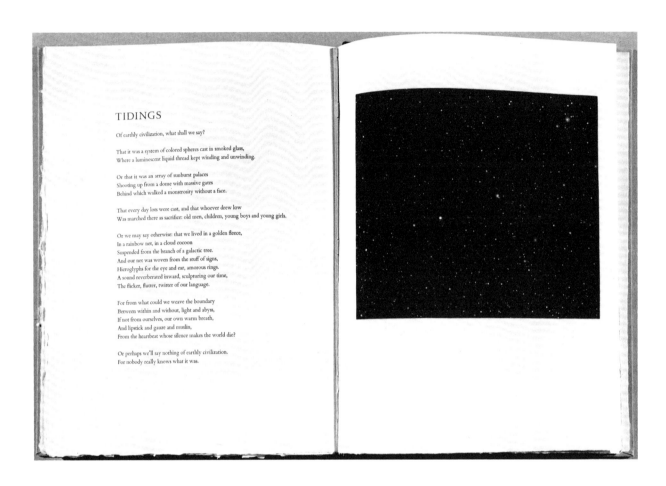

VIJA CELMINS
American, born Latvia 1939

The View by Czeslaw Milosz
New York, Library Fellows of the Whitney Museum
    of American Art, 1985
4 mezzotints, 14¾ × 11 inches each page
Edition 120
Collection Library of the Whitney Museum of
    American Art, New York

■ When approached by the Whitney Museum of American Art's publishing program, Latvian-born artist Vija Celmins proposed illustrating the writings of Lithuanian-born Nobel laureate Czeslaw Milosz. In the only instance in which previously or soon-to-be published texts[25] were allowed in its Artists and Writers Series, the Whitney accepted Celmins's choice of Milosz's *The View* (1985), a series of poems and prose meditations that seem to have been written expressly for Celmins. In spirit and meaning, Celmins's four exquisite mezzotints are the pictorial equivalents of Milosz's words. She juxtaposes familiar, commonplace subjects with the unknown: the planet Saturn; a tree adjacent to a star cluster, as seen from an antigravitational, bird's-eye perspective; a tree flanking a globe; and a galaxy. A fifth illustration reproduces Copernicus's sixteenth-century view of the universe in which the astronomer identified the sun as the center of a planetary system, with the earth revolving around it. Celmins's imaginary close-ups of celestial views make palpable such portions of the universe that could otherwise be overlooked. Printed on white paper, the illustrations are inserted closed bolt (accordion-bound) between text pages which are printed on gray paper and simply bound with a black leather spine.

BRUCE McLEAN
Scottish, born 1944

Dream Work by Mel Gooding
London, Knife Edge Press, 1985
24 screenprints, 16 × 12 inches each page
Edition 140
Collection Loriano Bertini

■ Although *Dream Work* (1985) begins with a quote from the seventeenth-century English author and physician, Sir Thomas Browne ("There is an art to making dreams, as well as their interpretations . . ."), the text consists of three cycles of poems by Mel Gooding: *In the Cold North*, *The Warm South*, and *Waking*. Bruce McLean designed the dramatic screenprints for every page of *Dream Work*, as well as one for the book jacket. Rapturous color is important to McLean's art. His expressionistic figuration uses the same elements repeatedly, combining ordinary things like ties, ladders, and shoes in fanciful ways. One gatefold portrays a seaside scene. Images follow references to color and objects—"Black shoes will be worn/ are necessary to the proper enjoyment of Art (the Italian influence—go for it!)." The poems follow the screenprints in the sequence of pages in the book.

Am Anfang ist das Ende
der Vulkan überhäuft uns mit Geschenken
wie traurig waren wir
der Himmel tropft auf die Teller
das Gras sinkt herab mit Tau bedeckt
Halleluja Schabernack und kein Ende
die Schelmen blasen die Schelmei
zaghaft liegen die Wasserrosen und schlagen
die Augen auf und zu
die Reusen sind leer
der schwarze Sack ist voll
was dem Apfel die Kerne sind der Erde die Ameisen
kein Geräusch ist hörbar
nur die Mondsichel steht am Himmel
das Feuerwerk knallt und die Nacht ist paillettenübersät.

MERET OPPENHEIM

Swiss, born Germany, 1913–1985

Caroline by Meret Oppenheim
Basel, Editions Fanal, 1985
21 etchings and 2 relief prints, 11 × 5½ inches each page
Edition 18
Courtesy Editions Fanal, Basel

■ In *Caroline* (1985), Meret Oppenheim orna-
mented her own short stories and poems with
intaglio prints. Two full-circle relief prints and
twenty-one delicate etchings, each composed in
a half-circle format opposite a short text, relate
to her descriptive writing that appears in two
languages—German and one French.

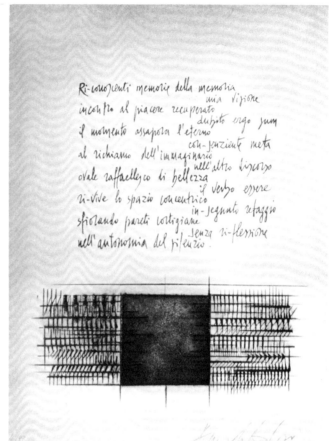

ARNALDO POMODORO
Italian, born 1926

De-Cantare Urbino by Miklos N. Varga
Introduction by Paolo Volponi, translated by Henry Martin
Pesaro, Edizioni della Pergola, 1985
8 color engravings, 17¾ × 13¼ inches each page
Bronze relief sculpture inset in cover of wood box,
    19 × 14½ × 1¼ inches
Edition 99
Courtesy Stephen Wirtz Gallery, San Francisco

■ It seems natural that sculptor Arnaldo Pomodoro created an illustrated book binding that alluded to his other three-dimensional works. For *De-Cantare Urbino* (1985), Pomodoro designed a triangular bronze relief which is set into the top of a wooden case. Eight engravings accompany a poetic text by Miklos N. Varga. Each page of the unbound folio combines a handwritten stanza and geometric figure (circle, square, triangle, or cube) printed in a single natural tone.

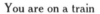
You are on a train

Travelling away from them

DONALD SULTAN

American, born 1951

Warm and Cold by David Mamet
New York, Solo Press Inc. and Joe Fawbush Editions, 1985
9 lithographs with *pochoir* and letterpress,
  21⅛ × 17⅛ inches each page
Edition 100
Courtesy Solo Press Inc., New York

■ *Warm and Cold* (1985) is the result of a collaboration between Donald Sultan and playwright David Mamet.[26] The text is a short, poignant poem (originally part of a letter from Mamet to Sultan) about their similar experiences of traveling for work and having to leave behind a beloved child. Both text and images are succinct and to the point: "You are on a train/ traveling away from them/ but they are thinking of you." Nine expressive line drawings in lithography, handcolored with *pochoir*, successfully interpret the author's poetic sentiments. Photographs of Sultan and Mamet's daughters, Frances and Willa, begin and end the book.

FRANCESCO CLEMENTE
Italian, born 1953

The Departure of the Argonaut by Alberto Savinio
London and New York, Petersburg Press, 1986
50 color lithographs, 26 × 20 inches each page
Edition 200
Courtesy Petersburg, London and New York

■ *The Departure of the Argonaut*, by Alberto Savinio[27] (1891–1952), written in 1917 in French, Italian, Latin, Greek, and German (and serialized in France and Germany the same year) is a travelogue and diary that recounts the writer's wartime experience, specifically his induction into the Italian army and his subse-quent departure by train and boat for the Salonika front. In 1918, *La Partenza dell' Argonauta* appeared in book form with related poetry, short tales, and theatre pieces, as the final and most autobiographical section of *Hermaphrodito*. Savinio patterned his humor-ous, nostalgic, and tragic tale after the Greek myth, *Argonautica* (3rd century B.C.), which chronicles the heroic voyage of Jason and the Argonauts in quest of the Golden Fleece. Illus-trated by Italian artist Francesco Clemente in 1983 and published in 1986, the story was newly translated into English by George Scrivani.[28]

Clemente approached each of five chapters and epilogue differently, obliquely wedding image to text. The artist does not depict specific incidents of the myth, but subtly balances the visual ideas—locomotives, ships, the sea, warriors, Roman ruins—with his own fantasy in the text folios. Clemente's energetic, figurative illustrations—upon, under, and around the printed text—spanning two pages without the interruption of a sewn gutter, are full of implied meaning. He utilizes repeated motifs, such as elaborate rope knots, brightly colored semaphore flags that spell out *Savinio*, and bright orange edging in the epilogue to extend the visual metaphors.

As this was the artist's first experience with planography, he experimented with an exten-sive range of lithographic techniques, using stones, aluminum plates, and treated mylar sheets, which allowed overlapping before the acetates were transferred to photosensitized plates. In addition to drawing with standard litho crayons and tusche, Clemente used graph-ite, graphite washes, rapidographs and ink, transfer paper, and various blotting methods to achieve a rich and varied display of effects. Printing was facilitated by a hand-inked, hand-fed offset proofing press which did not reverse the image. The unusual choice of lightweight Japanese Okawara paper and oversize format (26 × 39 inches; 65 × 100 cm, double-page) provided a large field and encouraged a lush, painterly approach. *The Departure of the Argonaut* is an extraordinary example of contemporary book making.[29]

"I am looking at Annie, I am looking at Gwen, I am looking at Lilly, I
am looking at Pam: I might join up with Pam and Gwen and hear the
voice that is new and cold and strange on the wind; I might join up with
Annie and live in the overwhelming blackness, which should then become
a permanent and essential part of my nature; I might try again to satisfy
Lilly, who is still an unending piece of parched earth longing for a
downpour; I might remain here, alone, in my part of the perfect place,
like a barge waiting for some piece of valuable cargo," said Tulip.

"Looking up, I see the elements do battle and take sides between day
and night; looking up, I see the moon, full but worn down like a much-
sucked peppermint in the broad daylight; looking up, I can feel the limit
of my own importance, I can feel the power of things that cannot be
brought to a quick conclusion," said Lilly.

"I am living both inside and outside the overwhelming blackness that is
a permanent and essential part of my nature, Umbra and Penumbra;
when Lilly, Pam, Gwen, and Tulip speak, I hear their voices, sometimes
as if delivered in a spiral, powered by a high wind, sometimes as if
delivered through a space that has an inferior field of gravity," said Annie.

"Again I hear the same voice on the wind, only now it surrounds us in
a circle. I see some large clouds—billowy, white, like wool only this
minute just fleeced from lambs—and I am lost in their slow and aimless
drift; I forget these clouds, billowy, white, might break suddenly, making
me long for our mother's lap and our father's lips after days of absence,"
said Pam.

ERIC FISCHL
American, born 1948

Annie, Gwen, Lilly, Pam and Tulip by Jamaica Kincaid
New York, Library Fellows of the Whitney Museum
  of American Art, 1986
9 lithographs, color and black-and-white,
  20 × 15 inches each page
Edition 145
Collection Library of the Whitney Museum of
  American Art, New York

■ When the Library Fellows of the Whitney
Museum of American Art asked Eric Fischl to
create the fourth illustrated book in their
Artists and Writers Series, he chose the work of
one of his favorite authors, Jamaica Kincaid.
Annie, Gwen, Lilly, Pam and Tulip (1986), a
previously unpublished short story written in
the dreamy, rhythmic style of a prose poem,
takes place on a hot Caribbean summer day.
Five young girls on the verge of womanhood
stare at the sky and muse about their future
and the nature of friendship, knowing they are
on the brink of change. "Jamaica's story," Fischl
commented, "might be [a] slumber party
where some girls wake up women, and some
don't."[30] Nine lithographs effectively capture
the exotic heat and latent sexuality of the
prose poem. Fischl begins the visual narrative
in black and white, moving into rich colors to
render suggestive scenes in loose wash strokes,
carefully pacing the flow of words with double-
page spreads and gatefolds. Fischl unites the
illustrations with the text by presenting images
specific to Kincaid's story as well as those that
seem to be evocative of its spirit.

The Times

Face across, dressed in white, connected to a body,
try to catch the eye, the intelligent contact
through the eye.
        Try to guess the destination
of train's nighttime ride.
        Man asks
if he can read my finished Times on seat next to me.

And slowly, the connection is there, that intellect
is eager for knowledge, news, poring, analyzing.
Just then Christ Church tower, lit in the night,
comes into view.
        But still there is the need
to satisfy, fulfill.
        Unceasing, painful
a little. The need to have satisfied
one's parents, to have given something back,
to a community.
        Then there is the painful
continuing, when others can no longer continue.
There are postcards, photos, in boxes, from friends
who will never again write (we can hope 'never'
is too strong): something they decided makes it
impossible, now.
        Yet other friends are coming,
and there is a party, and work.

She stays on, when I get off at Oxford. As I
walk down the platform, towards the barrier,
I turn once.

ALEX KATZ
American, born 1927

A Tremor in the Morning by Vincent Katz
New York, Peter Blum Edition , 1986
11 linocuts, 9¼ × 7½ inches each page;
10 woodcuts, 20½ × 19⅞ inches each page
Edition 300
Collection Alex Katz

■ A *Tremor in the Morning* (1986) is a collaboration between artist Alex Katz and his son Vincent. A suite of ten woodcut portraits of couples accompanies a book that includes eleven linocuts showing closeups of landscapes and cityscapes, and ten poems by Vincent Katz. For portrait subjects the artist turned to his family and friends (Jennifer Bartlett, Carter Ratcliff, Rackstraw Downes, and Katz's son Vincent and wife Ada) many of whom he had already portrayed in painting. Here he uses graphic media to achieve the final synthesis of form. Rather than gouging on a grained block, Katz favors a more open technique, utilizing line to interpret mass, reminiscent of prints by Felix Vallotton. Printed in a single flat color, faces are reduced to patterns of light and dark, with line often suggested rather than explicitly cut into the block. In some of the illustrations, the depiction of foreground and background planes is ambiguous.[31] Accompanying the prints is a small French-bound book (all pages are double-folded) set into a large white linen box beneath the portfolio. The poems, written in the language of everyday life, concern relationships, meetings, and partings. Linocuts of leaves, windows, and trees, all printed in beige and fuschia, seem more personal and romantic than the portraits, even though they demonstrate a similar degree of abstraction.

RONALD KING

British, born Brazil 1935

The Left-Handed Punch by Roy Fisher
Guildford, Circle Press, 1986
31 mixed-media prints, 15½ × 11½ inches each page
Edition 90
Collection Diane and Martin Ackerman

■ Ronald King started Circle Press in 1967. He is largely responsible for the current interest in artist-illustrated books among both British artists and collectors. *The Left-Handed Punch* (1986) is one of the most ambitious publications of the press, and is the fifth collaboration between poet Roy Fisher and Ronald King. The book introduces a new version of Punch and Judy. The handwritten text, with on-stage instructions and off-stage commentaries, is a four-sided monologue consisting of a prologue, six scenes, and an epilogue. Bawdy, comic, and macabre passages from *The Tragical Comedy or Comical Tragedy of Punch and Judy* (a script published by George Routledge & Sons in 1860) are disguised as footnotes. Twelve colorful puppets that fold out or move are attached to the ten French-folded sections. Tableau compositions and numerous vignettes utilizing photo collage, die-cutting, screenprinting, and lithography illustrate the dialogue. King designed a large aperture for the title blocking, cleverly suggestive of a puppet stage, for the slipcase cover.

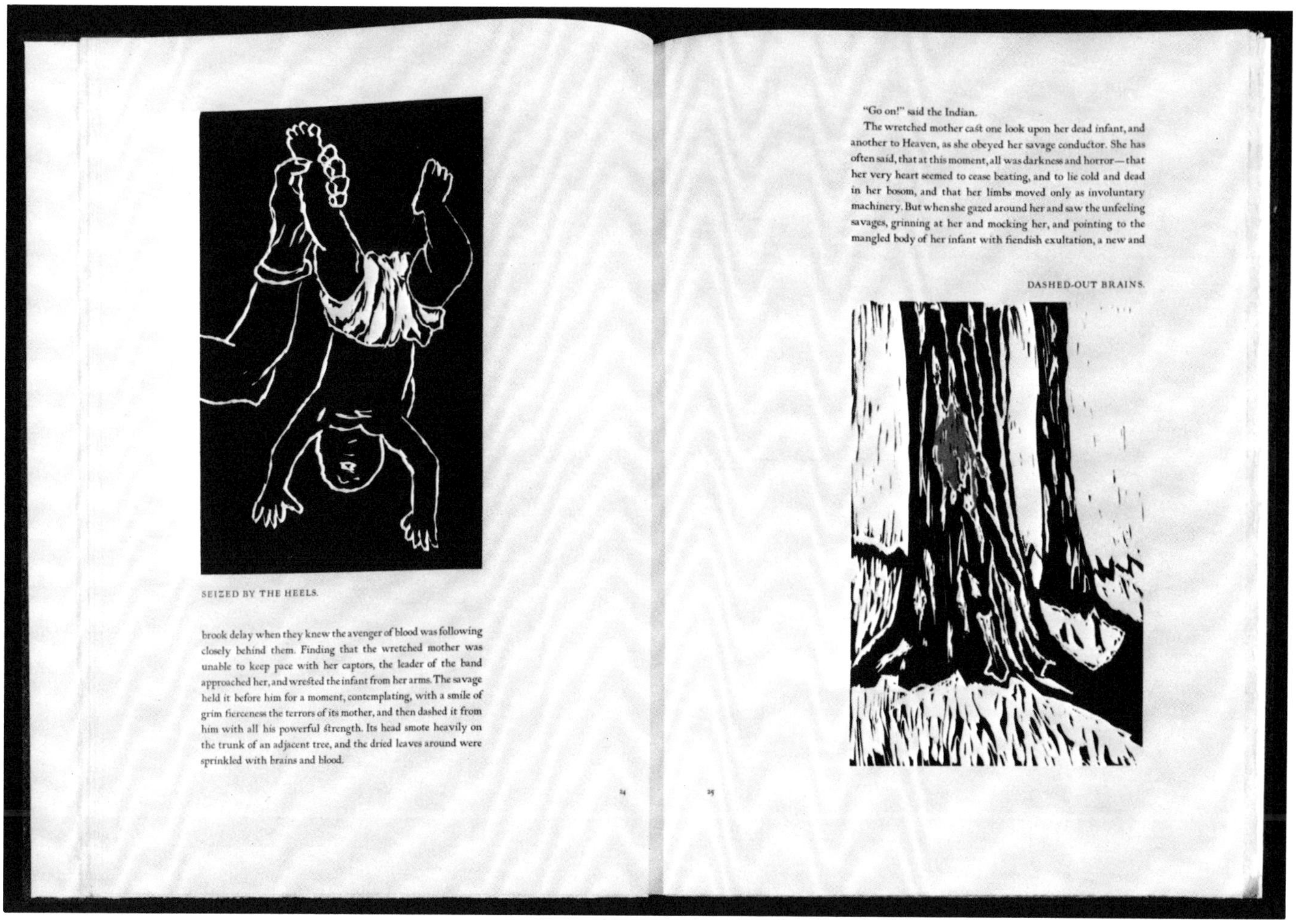

SEIZED BY THE HEELS.

brook delay when they knew the avenger of blood was following closely behind them. Finding that the wretched mother was unable to keep pace with her captors, the leader of the band approached her, and wrested the infant from her arms. The savage held it before him for a moment, contemplating, with a smile of grim fierceness the terrors of its mother, and then dashed it from him with all his powerful strength. Its head smote heavily on the trunk of an adjacent tree, and the dried leaves around were sprinkled with brains and blood.

"Go on!" said the Indian.

The wretched mother cast one look upon her dead infant, and another to Heaven, as she obeyed her savage conductor. She has often said, that at this moment, all was darkness and horror—that her very heart seemed to cease beating, and to lie cold and dead in her bosom, and that her limbs moved only as involuntary machinery. But when she gazed around her and saw the unfeeling savages, grinning at her and mocking her, and pointing to the mangled body of her infant with fiendish exultation, a new and

DASHED-OUT BRAINS.

RICHARD BOSMAN

Australian, born India 1944

Captivity Narrative of Hannah Duston related by Cotton Mather, John Greenleaf Whittier, Nathaniel Hawthorne and Henry David Thoreau

San Francisco, Arion Press, 1987

35 woodcuts, 16¾ × 12½ inches each page

Edition 400

Courtesy Arion Press, San Francisco

■ *Captivity Narrative of Hannah Duston*, first recorded in 1697, has impressed readers for more than two hundred years,[32] and is one of the earliest examples of the genre of American popular and moralizing literature. Arion Press developed the idea for this book, selecting four distinguished literary versions of the story as the basis of the text. The sixty-four-page bound volume, with thirty-five dramatic woodcuts by Australian painter Richard Bosman, appeared in 1987.

Because of Bosman's interest in violence, disasters, and despair, Arion Press suggested that he illustrate several incidents from Duston's life. Interspersed through the chronicles, his prints form their own parallel narrative, making the story seem less remote and creating another level of understanding for the reader. Captions telegraph events: "The Foe Close at Hand;" "Hand in Hand, Hushing Sobs:" "Sprinkled with Blood." Bosman includes pivotal incidents such as marauding Indians, the escape of the Duston children, Hannah's hand holding a hatchet. He portrays night scenes with a dark background and white line; he depicts daylight in reverse. The simplicity and directness of Bosman's woodblocks combine the diagrammatic renderings of naive art of the colonial period with bold Expressionist strokes.

LAUGHING WATER

Dvořák didn't like interrupting his stay in Spillville. The place suited him. But there were invitations. To Chicago to see the World's Fair; Otilka and another of his daughters went with him there. To Omaha and to St. Paul. On this trip he left the children behind and travelled with Mrs. Dvořák.

From St. Paul, where the large Czech community gave him a bigger welcome than he really wanted, he took a buggy ride over to Minneapolis to stand by the real object of his trip, the Falls of Minnehaha. "It is so intensely beautiful that words cannot describe it," he wrote home.

He wanted to write an opera based on Longfellow's *The Song of Hiawatha*. He had read the poem in translation. Naturally, its admiration for the indigenous culture appealed to Dvořák. So did Longfellow's lyrical, if rather didactic, restatement of landscape and the beauties of nature. Dvořák never found a good libretto, and the project fizzled. He stood by the falls, asked Kovařík for a pencil (nobody had any paper), and wrote something on his cuffs. It was the theme for the Sonatina, Opus 100, a piece he wrote later, after he left Spillville.

Dvořák loved the gash in the landscape, the great outpouring a waterfall is, and on the way back to New York the family stopped at Niagara where, of course, he was even more impressed than by the decorous Minnehaha, Laughing Water.

He wanted those big, bellowy sounds, too, not just the small voices of birds, the spirit whoosh of wind. He used to stand outside the train station in Prague and is said to have known the time of each train and, what is more unusual, the number of every locomotive. To his ear, each engine had a distinct tone. Engines, the sound of them, their big, pounding hearts. Get it down on the cuffs.

He left St. Paul and returned with his wife to Spillville where their children were waiting. The medicine show was still there. It was September 7, the day before his birthday.

[34]

STEVEN SORMAN

American, born 1948

Spillville by Patricia Hampl
Minneapolis, Milkweed Editions, 1987
27 engravings, 12 × 17 inches each page
Edition 150
Courtesy Milkweed Editions, Minneapolis

■ *Spillville* (1987), a collaboration between Steven Sorman and writer Patricia Hampl, contains twenty-seven lyrical engravings by Sorman and a collage of Hampl's short reflective essays, many of them about Antonin Dvořák and many, including the best of them, about Hampl herself. The theme for this project grew out of Hampl's interest in Dvořák and the working vacation the Czech composer took with his family during the summer of 1893 in a typically eccentric Midwestern community inhabited mostly by Bohemian immigrants.

In the spring of 1985 shortly after the centenary of Dvořák's sojourn in the heartland of the New World, Sorman and Hampl (with friends and family) traveled to Spillville, Iowa to recapture the romantic spirit of the Iowa landscape. Hampl's faithful description of the locale and milieu, which blends the personal and the historical (from Hampl's taped memories and the maestro's letters), is not unlike Dvořák's experience of transcribing the songs of the blue jays and scarlet tanagers, the roar of Minnehaha's waterfall, or the banjos and drums of the Kickapoo medicine show—which became elements of his Opus 96, the American Quartet. The natural grace of Sorman's luminous line engravings abstractly evokes the gently rolling landscape of northeastern Iowa, its hills, grasses, trees, winds, rivers, and waterfalls. The forty-one broadsheet pages, most of which contain a short prose meditation and engraving, are separated into three sections—Landscape, Studio, The Falls—and housed in a simple dark blue linen box. A variety of formats and visual relationships reveals itself as one moves the individual sheets from side to side in the unbound portfolio, each sheet visibly linked to the next in successive two-page spreads. Sorman and Hampl worked in tandem on the book's form and content, each respecting the integrity of the other's contribution. Together they have made a moving and memorable book.

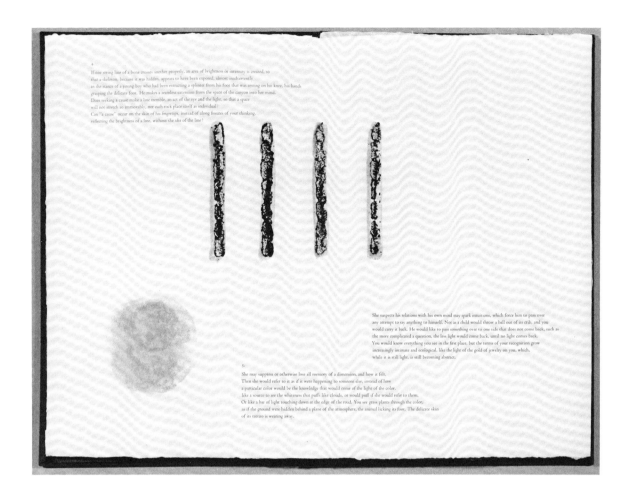

RICHARD TUTTLE
American, born 1941

Hiddenness by Mei-mei Berssenbrugge
New York, Library Fellows of the Whitney Museum
   of American Art, 1987
4 handstamped prints, 15 × 10 inches each page
Edition 120
Collection Library of the Whitney Museum of
   American Art, New York

■ *Hiddenness* (1987), with four handstamped prints by Richard Tuttle and Mei-mei Berssenbrugge's poem written in response to the images, is the extraordinary result of a publisher's thoughtful suggestion of a collaboration between an artist and a writer.[33] The seven sections of the prose poem relate to the imagery in an abstract way. In section six, for example, Berssenbrugge begins, "A creature walks on the quiet floor of the canyon, a dry floor, sparkling with mica, under which water flows, and turns its head aside from a thorny bush with red seeds hanging down." Later in the same paragraph Berssenbrugge refers to ". . . the ghost of an image . . . made to appear in his mind." The corresponding illumination on blue paper embedded with a faint white circle has oval imprints grouped in threes and inked in dark brown, ochre, and burnt umber, suggestive of pawprints. Tuttle designed the book with double-page spreads of images and verse. The handmade paper is molded with predetermined color areas on which images made by the inked sculptural tools are printed.[34]

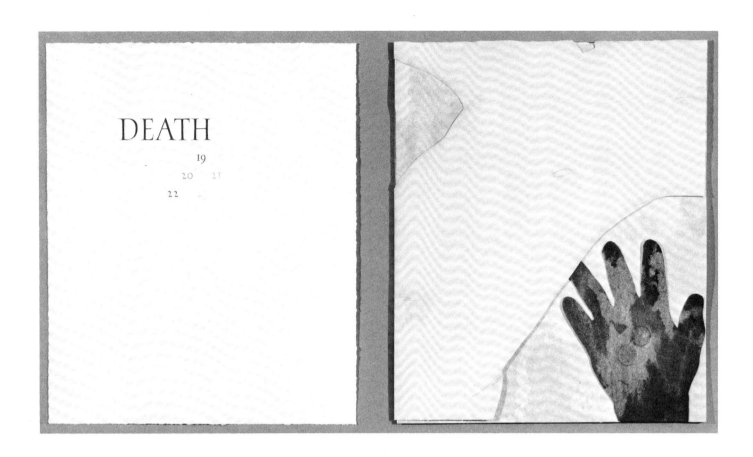

DEATH

19
20 21
22

SUSAN WEIL AND
MARJORIE VAN DYKE
Americans, born 1930 and 1956

The Epiphanies by James Joyce
New York, Vincent Fitz Gerald & Co., 1987
64 mixed-media prints with hand work,
    14 × 12 inches each page
Edition 50
Courtesy Vincent Fitz Gerald & Co., New York

■ Susan Weil and Marjorie Van Dyke's interpretation of James Joyce's *The Epiphanies*, published by Vincent Fitz Gerald in 1987, includes sixty-four graphically innovative etchings (employing more than one hundred plates), original watercolors, collage, and hand-cutting. Joyce considered these writings, many of which stemmed from his dreams, as intuitive revelations from daily life. Fitz Gerald's conception of the book is respectful to Joyce—everything rotates around his words. The book is designed so that phrases are read out of context and then brought into focus. The forty epiphanies are treated like poetry; they are printed separately in black with large type, their pagination individually color-coded by the artists' emotional responses to the writing. The collection is divided into four sections: *Death* and *Planes*, illuminated by Susan Weil, begin and end the series and are sewn signatures; *Games* and *Dreams*, rendered by Marjorie Van Dyke, are accordion-folded. The title page, in which Joyce's eyes become his glasses, is a

double-spread original collage of images from all four sections of the book. A title page with clusters of color-keyed numerals like flowers also introduces each section, establishing a rhythmic symmetry. Weil and Van Dyke tried to make their own visual metaphors, layerings, and symbols a counterpoint to Joyce's creative process. For Weil, "*The Epiphanies* are a wonderful insight into the writer's mind and methods."[35] *Death* begins with a hand holding two pennies (to place over a corpse's eyes).[36] The hand folds down and metamorphoses on the following page into the tail of a gray fish which is transformed ultimately into a pair of dancing nudes. Weil "tried to build a flowing image that spoke to the sorrows and terrors of these five epiphanies, with images from each woven into a whole. For me . . . the dream of Georgie dancing has the beauty of a child's spirit and also the reality of being Joyce's dream of his brother after death. It holds a feeling of joy and sorrow. The heart of feeling which is very much at one with the epiphany."[37]

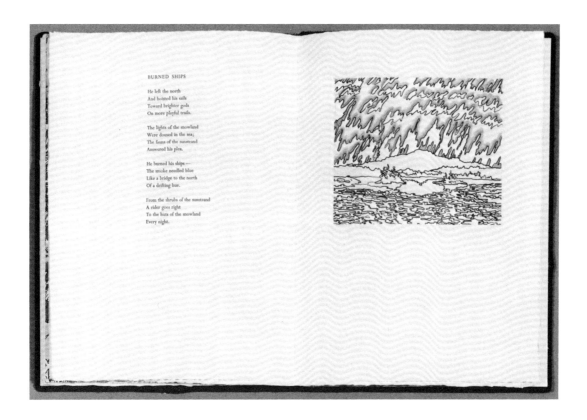

NEIL WELLIVER

American, born 1929

Henrik Ibsen Poems translated by Michael Feingold
New York, Vincent Fitz Gerald & Co., 1987
1 lithograph, 5 etchings, 8½ × 11½ inches each page
Edition 75
Courtesy Vincent Fitz Gerald & Co., New York

■ Henrik Ibsen, known by English-speaking audiences as one of the world's most influential dramatists, is celebrated in Scandinavia as one of the region's foremost nineteenth-century poets. Michael Feingold's new translation, *Henrik Ibsen Poems* (1987), collects twenty of the writer's finest works from his early adulthood, many never before published in English. The poems reveal various aspects of Ibsen's character—satirist, lover, philosopher, singer of nature and the outdoors, and the suffering soul of Romanticism—with clarity.

Vincent Fitz Gerald, the book's publisher, played a primary role in orchestrating the overall conception, design, and production of the book, as he does with all the *livres d'artiste* he publishes. He first conceived the project as a book illustrated with photographs. After recognizing the romantic basis of the poems, he realized that landscape painter Neil Welliver would provide a more appropriate visual accompaniment to the text.

Welliver's five color etchings and large double gatefold lithograph move from literal to abstract landscape, ending with a brilliant depiction of the northern lights. While the prints correspond to specific poems, they also have a symbolic overlay. For the long narrative poem "The Murder of Abraham Lincoln," Welliver created one of his rare portraits.[38] Welliver's majestic lithograph of a rocky, wooded Maine landscape bears a strong resemblance to the Scandinavian vistas celebrated by Ibsen. Inspired by the Scandinavian craft traditon, Fitz Gerald also commissioned weaver Sara Dochow to create an unusual, but fitting, handwoven and collaged silk binding in deep, resonant colors. The bound volume is enclosed in a red silk box.

JOHN BALDESSARI

American, born 1931

The Life and Opinions of Tristram Shandy, Gentleman
  by Laurence Sterne
Essay by Melvyn New
3 volumes
San Francisco, Arion Press, 1988
39 photo collages, 6¾ × 10¼ inches each page
Edition 400
Courtesy Arion Press, San Francisco

■ John Baldessari's illustrated version of Laurence Sterne's bawdy and licentious eighteenth-century novel, *The Life and Opinions of Tristram Shandy, Gentleman*, appeared in 1988.

Published by Arion Press in an elegant, three-volume slipcased set, the deluxe edition includes a facsimile of the complete 620-page text, a critical essay by Sterne scholar Dr. Melvyn New of the University of Florida, and an accordion-bound volume of Baldessari's thirty-nine double-page photo collages which can be viewed as two-page spreads or unfolded to an almost forty-foot length. While 'Shandean' quotes invest Baldessari's visual accompaniment with subtle historicism, the artist's carefully composed photo collages from cropped and rearranged press photographs, movie stills, documentary shots, and other sources (most of which date from the late 1950s and early 1960s) present *Tristram Shandy* in modern dress. Baldessari's brilliantly-colored seals that obscure faces function like Sterne's deliberate use of grammatical and typographic devices to arouse interest, withhold information, and imply moral censure. The photo lithographs are printed in rich duotone black, with overlays and tints of as many as seven colors.

The wit and sophistication of *Tristram*

Shandy appealed to Baldessari. He also liked the way Sterne visualized his book in pictorial terms, especially his unconventional approach to the printed page—the use of drawings, strangely-placed italics, brackets, pointing fingers, asterisks (sometimes several lines of them), totally blank pages, a black page, and a marbled page—which he recognized as not unlike some of his own recent work in film, video, and photography.[39] Sterne's insertion of stage directions and commentaries throughout the text, and the lack of a conventional, orderly narrative and chronological sequence (because of Tristram's interruptions, and musing digressions from plot or character)[40] also relate to Baldessari's own non-linear visual poetry. Baldessari's intense involvement with one of his favorite books has produced a creative metamorphosis. "As I read *Tristram* and worked on the art, it seemed more and more like he was my doppelgänger, or vice versa—that we were very similar spirits. At this point, I have enough material to do three volumes. The whole project has me very excited."[41]

a wicked heart. If you didn't keep your eye on your pretty pony it would jump the fence and be out of sight and you'd have to take your rope bridle and go after it, a trip that was sometimes short but was apt to turn your bones into a rack nonetheless.

Grandpa said Arthur Osgood had cheated. He was supposed to hide his eyes against the dead elm by the chopping block for a full minute, which he would time by counting to sixty. This would give Clivey (so Grandpa had always called him, and he hadn't minded, although he thought he would rearrange the teeth of a man—maybe even of a woman—who would call him that past the age of twelve) and the others a fair chance to hide. Clivey had still been looking for a place when Arthur Osgood got to sixty, turned around, and "caught him out" as he was trying to squirm—as a last resort—behind a pile of apple crates stacked haphazardly in the angle formed by the barn and the press-shed, where the machine that pressed blems into cider bulked in the dimness like an engine of torture.

"It wasn't fair," Grandpa said. "You didn't do no bitching about it and that was right, because a man never does no bitch-ing—they call it bitching because it ain't for men or even boys smart enough to know better and brave enough to do better. Just the same, it wasn't fair. I can say that now because you didn't say it then."

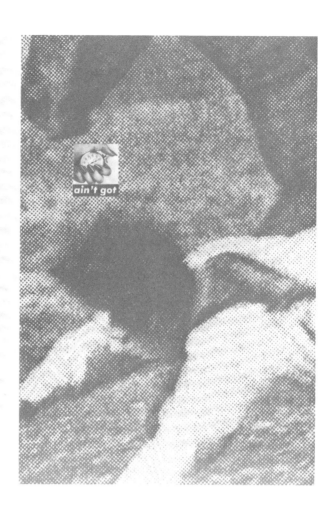

BARBARA KRUGER

American, born 1945

My Pretty Pony by Stephen King
New York, Library Fellows of the Whitney Museum
    of American Art, 1988
9 color lithographs, 20¼ × 13¾ inches each page
Stainless steel cover with digital clock
Edition 250
Collection Library of the Whitney Museum of
    American Art, New York

■ Sponsored by the Library Fellows of the Whitney Museum of American Art, *My Pretty Pony* (1988) pairs writer Stephen King with Barbara Kruger, an artist known for her appropriation of commercial art techniques and tabloid clichés. When the Library Fellows asked Kruger to create a book, she expressed interest in Angelica Carter, Elmore Leonard, and Stephen King, all of whom have enormous mass-market appeal. Kruger and King never actually met. Whitney Museum Librarian May Castleberry acted as intermediary and had all but given up hope that legal and contractual problems could be worked out when King sent her the thirty-five-page manuscript.

In King's previously unpublished and moving short story, a sick old farmer rapidly approach-ing the end of his days lovingly gives his adoring youngest grandson, Clivey, his silver pocket watch and instructs him on the nature of time, its irregular passing and cruel tricks. The book's title, which appears emblazoned at the beginning, middle, and end of the book in large bold helvetica letters silkscreened in white on red, is a metaphor for the perception of time—"pretty, but with a wicked heart." Kruger's nine lithographs, which are drawn from three compelling, cropped and framed photographs of horses and men, are blown up to exaggerate the grain of the film until the Ben Day dot-screen becomes indecipherable. The lithographs are alternately printed in black, red, and blue. Their relationship to the text is elliptical. They are bound into the volume on the right-hand page of a two-page spread after every five pages of text. On each illustration is a small square inset of a woman's hand punching a stop watch and a fragment of a key phrase from the text: "Time ain't got nothing to do with how fast you count."

Barbara Kruger designed the elegant book with a red leather spine and polished stainless steel covers. No printing mars the sleek, industrial look of the binding. The front is inset with a functional Big Time digital clock which is expected to last through 1990; its eventual failure is a property of the book. In her thoughtful collaboration with King, Kruger has abstracted the essence from his parable, focus-ing on time—the subject of the book—so that it can be understood viscerally as well as intellectually.

Notes

[1] A pencil drawing, included in this exhibition, with alternate schemes for die-cutting the book is only one of more than a hundred examples of technical papers used in the complex production of this volume.

[2] David Hockney toyed with the idea of illustrating *Grimm's Fairy Tales* for years (he did an etching of Rumpelstiltskin in 1961). In 1967, after completing the illustrations for an edition of poems (*Illustrations for Thirteen Poems for C. P. Cavafy*), Hockney read more than two hundred fairy tales, finally culling his favorites to a more manageable number at the suggestion of his publisher Paul Cornwall-Jones. Hockney made his selections because of the visual images suggested by the stories. *Old Rinkrank*, for example, begins, "A King built a glass mountain. . . ." Hockney acknowledged that he was compelled by the idea of drawing a glass mountain. "When I read it, I just couldn't resist the idea of doing it and giving myself the problem," he confessed. "Grimm's have been done by a lot of people. But . . . most of them usually choose the most dramatic parts . . . I didn't want to do that. I wanted to build up the illustrations and the story by using details. (Quote from *David Hockney: Grimm's Fairy Tales*, exhibition brochure (London: Victoria and Albert Museum, n.d.).)

[3] The English translations were originally published by the University of California Press in 1958.

[4] From an unpublished letter from Terry Allen to Joan Tewksbury in 1980, as published in Marcia Tucker, "Terry Allen [on everything]," *Artforum* XIV (October, 1980), pp. 42–49.

[5] See Christian Geelhaar, *Jasper Johns Working Proofs* (London and New York: Petersburg Press, 1980), p. 39.

[6] *Glittering Remains* can be compared to the original copperplate included in this exhibition.

[7] Published by Giulio Einaudi, Turin.

[8] Susan Taylor, "A Conversation with Giulio Paolini," *Print Collector's Newsletter* XV, 5 (November–December, 1984), p. 169.

[9] In April 1972, Tatyana Grosman learned that writer and filmmaker Alain Robbe-Grillet was lecturing at New York University's Maison Française. She had just read a Robbe-Grillet novel and had been struck by his use of repetition, which reminded her of Robert Rauschenberg. (See Tony Towle, "Rauschenberg: Two Collaborations—Robbe-Grillet and Voznesensky," *Print Collector's Newsletter* X, 2 (May–June, 1979), pp. 37–41.) When Robbe-Grillet mentioned Rauschenberg in his lecture, Grosman considered her intuition valid and approached the writer about a project for ULAE. A working plan was set in motion; lithographic plates were sent to France where Robbe-Grillet would handwrite a chapter of the text. The plates were returned to West Islip, New York, where they were proofed on a hand-fed offset press (which did not reverse the image) and Robbe-Grillet's official English translator Richard Howard transcribed the pages for Rauschenberg. The artist responded with images, proofs of which were sent back to Robbe-Grillet with more plates. An ongoing dialogue was established. This transfer occurred five times in six years, resulting in *Traces suspectes en surface*.

[10] See parenthetical reference above in note 9 to Tony Towle's article, p. 38.

[11] *Contemporary Artists' Books Catalogue* (London: Eaton House Publishers Ltd., 1979), p. 24.

[12] Letter from Michael Kidner to the author, January 10, 1988.

[13] This collaboration is the result of a fortuitous meeting deftly engineered by Tatyana Grosman. From the beginning of her career, Mrs. Grosman insisted on using unpublished writings. In October 1978, Doubleday & Company, New York, published a compendium of Voznesensky's recent work with the same title, which included an edited version of the original poem.

[14] *Unforgettable Fire* was published in New York by Pantheon in 1981.

[15] Ellen G. D'Oench and Jean E. Feinberg, *Jim Dine Prints 1977–1985* (New York: Harper & Row, 1986), p. 15.

[16] The first thirty deluxe copies of this book include a watercolor, shown in this exhibition.

[17] Letter from Albert Dupont to the author, January 20, 1988.

[18] William C. Seitz, *The Art of Assemblage* (New York: The Museum of Modern Art, 1961), p. 13.

[19] Also on view in this exhibition are the copperplate and color proof from which the etched images originated.

[20] The extraordinary sympathy these men had for each other's ideas is not surprising. Both men have written extensively about art. Both were profoundly affected by the Spanish Civil War. As a Loyalist, Alberti chose exile in Buenos Aires, Paris, and Rome during the thirty-five years of the Franco regime. Unable to return to Spain, memories and images of his home haunted him. The war did not directly affect Motherwell, an American, but Spain's moral struggle became one of the central metaphors of his art.

[21] A trade edition of *Inferno* was published in 1985 by Thames and Hudson, London and New York.

[22] Tom Phillips, *Dante's Inferno translated, illustrated and designed by Tom Phillips at Talfourd Press, London. 1983* (London: Waddington Galleries, 1983).

[23] Some editions of the book (not included in the exhibition) were elegantly bound in three volumes by Pella Erskine-Tulloch in 1986. Included in the exhibition is *A TV Dante* (1985), a video of a television pilot made for Channel 4 in Great Britain in collaboration with film director Peter Greenaway.

[24] In addition to the book, the exhibition includes a mock-up of a double-page spread and accompanying letterpress cuts for the application of color.

[25] The texts are from Milosz's *Bells in Winter* (1978) and *Notes & Inscripts* (1984).

[26] Playwright David Mamet included the short, poignant poem that later became the text of *Warm and Cold* in a letter to Donald Sultan. (Mamet is the godfather of Sultan's daughter.) When Sultan mentioned the poem to Joe Fawbush, the publisher recognized the potential of a collaboration between Mamet and Sultan.

[27] Albert Savinio was a little-known proto-modernist poet, playwright, composer, painter, and set designer. He was the brother of the metaphysical artist Giorgio de Chirico.

[28] The source of Scrivani's translation was the Supercoralli edition, published by Giulio Einaudi Editore, Turin, in 1981.

[29] Two stage proofs for Chapter V, which date from 1983 but were not used to illustrate the text, are also on view in this exhibition, as is a special book jacket designed in 1986 and released as a single print (*Untitled B*).

[30] Gerald Marzorati, "Fischl and Kincaid," *Vanity Fair* (December 1986), p. 140.

[31] This exhibition also includes two basswood blocks: *Alex and Ada* and *Peter and Linda*.

[32] The full title of the work in the version included here is *Captivity Narrative of Hannah Duston related by Cotton Mather, John Greenleaf Whittier, Nathaniel Hawthorne and Henry David Thoreau*. The gruesome tale is as follows. During an Indian attack on Haverhill, Massachusetts, Hannah Duston, who had just given birth to her eighth child, was unable to escape with her husband and family. The Indians slaughtered the newborn child, captured Duston and the midwife, and forced them on a long march into the wilderness. The two women became part of an Indian clan for six weeks until they were able to kill their captors and return to civilization. While viewed by her contemporaries as a heroine, Duston's actions were reevaluated in the succeeding years—especially since ten of her own victims were women and children. The story was first recorded by the Puritan moralist Cotton Mather who published three different accounts, all defending her vengeance as a righteous act. A hundred years later, Quaker poet John Greenleaf Whittier criticized Duston's aggressive behavior, but acknowledged that terror and grief caused temporary insanity. Nathaniel Hawthorne condemned Duston as a murderess. But Henry David Thoreau took a more dispassionate view, retelling Hannah's escape along the Merrimack as part of the account of his own journey on the same river in *A Week on the Concord and Merrimack Rivers*.

[33] The publisher's introduction eventually resulted in a marriage between the artist and the writer.

[34] A preparatory drawing and four sculptural tools carved by the artist show the early phase of the realization of this handsome accordion-bound volume.

[35] From undated letter from Susan Weil to Vincent Fitz Gerald.

[36] A maquette and plates for *Death* are also included in the exhibition.

[37] From undated letter from Susan Weil to Vincent Fitz Gerald.

[38] A drawing, copperplates, and tap outs for this portrait are included in the exhibition and demonstrate aspects of the artist's working process.

[39] Gerrit Henry, "John Baldessari, Gentleman," *Print Collector's Newsletter* (May–June, 1989), p. 51.

[40] Ibid.

[41] Ibid., p. 53.

CHECKLIST OF THE EXHIBITION

Height precedes width precedes depth; unless otherwise noted, all dimensions given below refer to the size of a single page.

TERRY ALLEN

American, born 1943

Juarez
Chicago, Landfall Press, 1976
6 lithographs, 13¼ × 13¼ inches each page
33 rpm record
Edition 50
Courtesy Landfall Press, Chicago and New York

Ancillary material:
Bed with Ditch, from *Juarez*, 1976
Lithograph, 13¼ × 13¼ inches
Courtesy Landfall Press, Chicago and New York

Ditch with Heart, from *Juarez*, 1976
Lithograph, 13¼ × 13¼ inches
Courtesy Landfall Press, Chicago and New York

DOTTY ATTIE

American, born 1938

Mother's Kisses
New York, Solo Press Inc., 1982
26 handcolored images and words, 6 × 6 inches each page
1 lithograph, 35¾ × 26½ inches
Edition 32
Courtesy Solo Press Inc., New York

JOHN BALDESSARI

American, born 1931

The Life and Opinions of Tristram Shandy, Gentleman
   by Laurence Sterne
Essay by Melvyn New
3 volumes
San Francisco, Arion Press, 1988
39 photo collages, 6¾ × 10¼ inches each page
Edition 400
Courtesy Arion Press, San Francisco

MARK BEARD

American, born 1956

The Côte d'Azur Triangle by Harry Kondoleon
New York, Vincent Fitz Gerald & Co., 1985
7 color lithographs, 11 etchings,
   14⅛ × 12⅛ inches each page
Edition 119
Courtesy Vincent Fitz Gerald & Co., New York

RICHARD BOSMAN

Australian, born India 1944

Captivity Narrative of Hannah Duston related by Cotton Mather,
   John Greenleaf Whittier, Nathaniel Hawthorne and Henry
   David Thoreau
San Francisco, Arion Press, 1987
35 woodcuts, 16¾ × 12½ inches each page
Edition 400
Courtesy Arion Press, San Francisco

DANIEL BUREN

French, born 1938

D'une impression l'autre
Neuchâtel, Editions Media and the Artist, 1983
30 serigraphs and 30 color photographs,
   13⅛ × 20½ inches each page
Edition 95
Courtesy of the artist

POL BURY

Belgian, born 1922

Piccola guida all' uso di un viaggiatore in Italia
   by Maurice Stendhal
Milan, Sergio Tosi Stampatore, 1967
10 lithographs, 18½ × 14⅝ inches each page
Edition 130
Collection Loriano Bertini

PATRICK CAULFIELD

British, born 1936

Some Poems of Jules Laforgue
London, Petersburg Press, 1973
22 silkscreens, 16 × 14 inches each page
Edition 500
Collection Diane and Martin Ackerman

VIJA CELMINS

American, born Latvia 1939

The View by Czeslaw Milosz
New York, Library Fellows of the Whitney Museum
   of American Art, 1985
4 mezzotints, 14¾ × 11 inches each page
Edition 120
Collection Library of the Whitney Museum of
   American Art, New York

FRANCESCO CLEMENTE

Italian, born 1953

The Departure of the Argonaut by Alberto Savinio
London and New York, Petersburg Press, 1986
50 color lithographs, 26 × 20 inches each page
Edition 200
Courtesy Petersburg, London and New York

Ancillary material:
Untitled B, 1986
Lithograph, 26 × 80 inches
Courtesy Petersburg, London and New York

Untitled (stage proof for Chapter V), *The Departure
   of the Argonaut*, 1983–1986
Lithograph, 17 × 14 inches
Courtesy Petersburg, London and New York

Untitled (stage proof for Chapter V), *The Departure of the Argonaut*, 1983–1986
Lithograph, 17 × 14 inches
Courtesy Petersburg, London and New York

JIM DINE
American, born 1935

The Apocalypse: The Revelation of St. John the Divine
San Francisco, Arion Press, 1982
29 woodcuts, 15 × 11¼ inches each page
Edition 150
Courtesy of the artist

ALBERT DUPONT
French, born 1951

Nathalie et Justine
Paris, L'Inéditeur, 1983
Book/object, 5½ × 9 × 2¾ inches
Edition 24
Courtesy L'Inéditeur, Paris

Ancillary materials:
Copperplate, 12¼ × 14¼ inches
Courtesy L'Inéditeur, Paris

Color etching, 12¼ × 14¼ inches
Courtesy L'Inéditeur, Paris

ERIC FISCHL
American, born 1948

Annie, Gwen, Lilly, Pam and Tulip by Jamaica Kincaid
New York, Library Fellows of the Whitney Museum
    of American Art, 1986
9 lithographs, color and black-and-white,
    20 × 15 inches each page
Edition 145
Collection Library of the Whitney Museum of
    American Art, New York

LUCIO FONTANA
Italian, 1899–1968

Portrait d' Antonin Artaud by Otto Hahn
Paris, Editions du Soleil Noir, 1968
Book and two of four multiples housed in painted
    wood box-sculpture

Book: 7¾ × 5¾ inches; each multiple: 7⅜ × 5 11/16 inches;
    wood box-sculpture (closed): 14⅜ × 9⅜ × 2 9/16 inches
Edition 80
Collection The Museum of Modern Art, New York. Monroe
    Wheeler Fund.   932.69.

R. BUCKMINSTER FULLER
American, 1895–1983

Tetrascroll by R. Buckminster Fuller
West Islip, New York, Universal Limited Art Editions, 1976
21 color lithographs, 30 11/16 × 35⅜ inches each page
Edition 34
Collection Nancy and Edwin Marks

JOHN FURNIVAL
British, born 1933

Blind Date by Thomas Meyer
Guildford, Circle Press, 1979
10 etchings and embossed prints including 1 color etching
    and aquatint, 11 × 11 inches each page
Edition 335
Collection Diane and Martin Ackerman

WOLFGANG GAFGEN
German, born 1936

En Bas by Olivier Kaeppelin
Paris, Editions Baudoin Lebon, 1984
15 intaglios, 13¾ × 15¾ inches each page
Edition 90
Courtesy Galerie Baudoin Lebon, Paris

MARCO GASTINI
Italian, born 1938

Pantomima by Ugo Leonzio
Genoa, Franco Mello & Giorgio Persano Editori, 1977
21 lithographs and serigraphs,
    13⅞ × 19¾ inches each page
Edition 40
Collection Loriano Bertini

DAVID HOCKNEY
British, born 1937

Six Fairy Tales from the Brothers Grimm
    translated by Heiner Bastian
Edition D
London, Petersburg Press, 1969
39 etchings, 17½ × 12⅛ inches each page
Edition 400
Courtesy Petersburg, London and New York

Ancillary material:
*The Princess in Her Tower, Six Fairy Tales from the Brothers
    Grimm*, 1969
Etching, 17½ × 12⅛ inches
Courtesy Petersburg, London and New York

*The Enchantress with the Baby Rapunzel, Six Fairy Tales from
    the Brothers Grimm*, 1969
Etching, 17½ × 12⅛ inches
Courtesy Petersburg, London and New York

*The Sexton Disguised as a Ghost Stood Still as a Stone, Six
    Fairy Tales from the Brothers Grimm*, 1969
Etching, 17½ × 12⅛ inches
Courtesy Petersburg, London and New York

*The Haunted Castle, Six Fairy Tales from the Brothers
    Grimm*, 1969
Etching, 17½ × 12⅛ inches
Courtesy Petersburg, London and New York

*The Glass Mountain, Six Fairy Tales from the Brothers
    Grimm*, 1969
Etching, 17½ × 12⅛ inches
Courtesy Petersburg, London and New York

*The Black Cat Leaping, Six Fairy Tales from the Brothers
    Grimm*, 1969
Etching, 17½ × 12⅛ inches
Courtesy Petersburg, London and New York

GOTTFRIED HONEGGER
Swiss, born 1917

Zitat by Max Frisch
Zurich, Verlag 3, 1976
7 woodcuts, 8⅝ × 7 1/16 inches each page
Edition 100
Courtesy Verlag 3, Zurich

JASPER JOHNS
American, born 1930

Foirades/Fizzles by Samuel Beckett
London and New York, Petersburg Press, 1976
33 etchings, 13¹⁄₁₆ × 9 ¹⁵⁄₁₆ inches each page
Cover, 1 serigraph, and 1 lithograph, 13¹⁄₁₆ × 9 ¹⁵⁄₁₆ inches
Edition 250
Courtesy Petersburg, London and New York

Ancillary material:
Words (Buttock, Knee, Sock . . .), from Chapter 1,
    Foirades/Fizzles, 1976
Etching and aquatint, 13¹⁄₁₆ × 19⅞ inches
Courtesy Petersburg, London and New York

Four Variations on Untitled (ABCD; BCDA; CDAB; DABC),
    from Chapter 1, *Foirades/Fizzles*, 1976
Etching and aquatint, 13¹⁄₁₆ × 19⅞ inches
Courtesy Petersburg, London and New York

Torse, from Chapter 3, *Foirades/Fizzles*, 1976
Serigraph and aquatint, 13¹⁄₁₆ × 19⅞ inches
Courtesy Petersburg, London and New York

Casts and Hatchings, from Chapter 2, *Foirades/Fizzles*, 1976
Etching and aquatint, 13¹⁄₁₆ × 19⅞ inches
Courtesy Petersburg, London and New York

Buttocks-Knee-Foothandsockfloor-Face-Torso, from Chapter 4,
    Foirades/Fizzles, 1976
Etching, 13¹⁄₁₆ × 19⅞ inches
Courtesy Petersburg, London and New York

Feet (A), from Chapter 4, *Foirades/Fizzles*, 1976
Aquatint, 13¹⁄₁₆ × 19⅞ inches
Courtesy Petersburg, London and New York

Handfootsockfloor, from Chapter 5, *Foirades/Fizzles*, 1976
Etching and aquatint, 13¹⁄₁₆ × 19⅞ inches
Courtesy Petersburg, London and New York

ALEX KATZ
American, born 1927

A Tremor in the Morning by Vincent Katz
New York, Peter Blum Edition , 1986
11 linocuts, 9¼ × 7½ inches each page;
10 woodcuts, 20½ × 19⅞ inches each page
Edition 300
Collection Alex Katz

Ancillary material:
2 woodblocks (*Ada and Alex* and *Peter and Linda*)
Basswood, 12 × 12 inches each
Collection The Brooklyn Museum, Gift of the artist   86.211.5,
    86.211.10

MICHAEL KIDNER
British, born 1917

The Elastic Membrane
Guildford, Circle Press, 1979
2 spiral-bound books: *Notebook*, 7⅞ × 6¾ inches;
    Continuity Book, 9¾ × 8¼ inches
6 prints: 3 photo etchings, 16¾ × 13 inches each page;
    3 continuous-tone lithographs,
    16½ × 13 inches each page
Multiple object, 17 × 13¼ × ⅞ inches
Malaysian plywood box with Perspex cover,
    17⁷⁄₁₆ × 14 × 2½ inches
Edition 300
Collection Diane and Martin Ackerman

RONALD KING
British, born Brazil 1935

The Left-Handed Punch by Roy Fisher
Guildford, Circle Press, 1986
31 mixed-media prints, 15½ × 11½ inches each page
Edition 90
Collection Diane and Martin Ackerman

BARBARA KRUGER
American, born 1945

My Pretty Pony by Stephen King
New York, Library Fellows of the Whitney Museum
    of American Art, 1988
9 color lithographs, 20¼ × 13¾ inches each page
Stainless steel cover with digital clock
Edition 250
Collection Library of the Whitney Museum of
    American Art, New York

SOL LₑWITT
American, born 1928

Ficciones by Jorge Luis Borges
New York, The Limited Editions Club, Ltd., 1984
22 serigraphs, 8 × 8 inches each page
Edition 1500
Courtesy The Limited Editions Club, Ltd., New York

ALEXANDER LIBERMAN
American, born Russia, 1912

Nostalgia for the Present by Andrei Voznesensky
West Islip, New York, Universal Limited Art Editions, 1979

Untitled page 15
Lithograph, 40⅞ × 27⅜ inches
Edition 12/28
Collection of the Grunwald Center for the Graphic Arts,
    University of California, Los Angeles, Gift of the Friends of
    the Graphic Arts and the UCLA Art Council in honor of E.
    Maurice Bloch

Untitled page 17
Lithograph, 41 × 27⅝ inches
Edition 12/28
Collection of the Grunwald Center for the Graphic Arts,
    University of California, Los Angeles, Gift of the Friends of
    the Graphic Arts and the UCLA Art Council in honor of E.
    Maurice Bloch

MARKUS LÜPERTZ
German, born 1941

Ich Stand vor der Mauer aus Glas by Markus Lüpertz
Berlin, Galerie Springer, 1982
10 color lithographs and 1 watercolor,
    16½ × 11 ¹⁵⁄₁₆ inches each page
Edition 220
Courtesy Galerie Springer, Berlin

BRUCE McLEAN
Scottish, born 1944

Dream Work by Mel Gooding
London, Knife Edge Press, 1985
24 screenprints, 16 × 12 inches each page
Edition 140
Collection Loriano Bertini

MATTA
(Roberto Antonio Sebastian Matta Echaurren)
Chilean, born 1911

Ubu Roi by Alfred Jarry
Paris, Dupont-Visat, L'Inéditeur, 1982
8 handcolored engravings, 16⅛ × 10¼ inches each page
Edition 165
Courtesy L'Inéditeur, Paris (Christine and Albert Dupont)

JOAN MIRÓ

Spanish, 1893–1983

Le Courtisan grotesque by Adrian de Monluc
Paris, Le Degré Quarante et Un, 1974
15 etchings with aquatint, 16½ × 11½ inches each page
Cover, 1 drypoint with aquatint, 16½ × 12⅜ inches
Edition 95
Courtesy Irving Zucker Art Books, New York

ROBERT MOTHERWELL

American, born 1915

El Negro by Rafael Alberti, translated by Vincente Lléo Cañal
Mount Kisco, New York, Tyler Graphics Ltd., 1983
19 lithographs, 15 × 15 inches; 15 × 25¾ inches;
    15 × 37¾ inches
Edition 51
Courtesy Tyler Graphics Ltd., Mount Kisco, New York

Ancillary materials:
Gypsy Curse, from *El Negro*, 1983
Two-color lithograph, chine appliqué, 15 × 15 inches
Edition 51
Courtesy Tyler Graphics Ltd., Mount Kisco, New York

Black Wall of Spain, from *El Negro*, 1983
Three-color lithograph, 15 × 37¾ inches
Edition 51
Courtesy Tyler Graphics Ltd., Mount Kisco, New York

Black with No Way Out, from *El Negro*, 1983
Three-color lithograph, 15 × 37¾ inches
Edition 51
Courtesy Tyler Graphics Ltd., Mount Kisco, New York

LOUISE NEVELSON

American, born Russia, 1900–1988

Nevelson's World by Jean Lipman
New York, Hudson Hills Press, Inc. and Pace Editions, 1983
1 seven-color serigraph, 13 × 12 inches
Black polyester-resin multiple on box cover,
    9⅝ × 8½ × ⁷⁄₁₆ inches
Edition 100
Courtesy Pace Editions, New York

MERET OPPENHEIM

Swiss, born Germany, 1913–1985

Caroline by Meret Oppenheim
Basel, Editions Fanal, 1985
21 etchings and 2 relief prints, 11 × 5½ inches each page
Edition 18
Courtesy Editions Fanal, Basel

GIULIO PAOLINI

Italian, born 1940

*Sei illustrazioni per gli scritti sull'Arte Antica di
    Johann J. Winckelmann*
Genoa, Franco Mello & Giorgio Persano Editori, 1977
6 serigraphs and lithographs,
    17 × 13⅜ inches each page
Edition 40
Collection Loriano Bertini

TOM PHILLIPS

British, born 1937

Inferno by Dante Alighieri
London, Talfourd Press, 1983
3 volumes
34 folios containing various combinations of etching,
    lithograph, and serigraph, 16⅜ × 12½ inches each page
Edition 85
Collection Tom Phillips

Ancillary material:
Peter Greenaway and Tom Phillips
A TV Dante, 1985
13½ minutes
Collection Richard Minsky

PABLO PICASSO

Spanish, 1881–1973

Le Cocu magnifique by Fernand Crommelynck
Paris, Atelier Crommelynck, 1968
7 etchings, 4 aquatints with etching, 1 aquatint with drypoint
    and etching, 11½ × 15 inches each page
Edition 200
Courtesy Irving Zucker Art Books, New York

ARNALDO POMODORO

Italian, born 1926

De-Cantare Urbino by Miklos N. Varga
Introduction by Paolo Volponi, translated by Henry Martin
Pesaro, Edizioni della Pergola, 1985
8 color engravings, 17¾ × 13¼ inches each page
Bronze relief sculpture inset in cover of wood box,
    19 × 14½ × 1¼ inches
Edition 99
Courtesy Stephen Wirtz Gallery, San Francisco

ROBERT RAUSCHENBERG

American, born 1925

Traces suspectes en surface by Alain Robbe-Grillet
West Islip, New York, Universal Limited Art Editions, 1978
36 color lithographs, 27 × 20 inches each page
Edition 36
Private collection

JUDY RIFKA

American, born 1945

Opera of the Worms by Rene Ricard
New York, Solo Press Inc. and Joe Fawbush Editions, 1984
15 color lithographs, 12 × 9 inches each page
Edition 80
Courtesy Solo Press Inc., New York

Ancillary material:
Paste-up
Mylar, 11 × 8½ inches
Courtesy Solo Press Inc., New York

5 photo-engraved letterpress plates
Magnesium mounted on pressboard, dimensions variable
Courtesy Solo Press Inc., New York

LARRY RIVERS

American, born 1923

The Donkey and the Darling by Terry Southern
West Islip, New York, Universal Limited Art Editions, 1977
52 color lithographs, 18½ × 21½ inches each page
Edition 35
Courtesy Rose Art Museum, Brandeis University,
    Waltham, Massachusetts   Anonymous Gift

LUCAS SAMARAS

American, born Greece, 1936

Book by Lucas Samaras
New York, Pace Editions, 1968
11 color serigraphs with offset, embossing,
　　thermography, die-cut, and collage mounted on masonite,
　　10 × 10 inches each page
Edition 100
Courtesy Pace Editions, New York

Ancillary material:
Sketch for cover of *Book*, 1967
Graphite pencil on paper, 8⁹⁄₁₆ × 11 inches
Collection The Museum of Modern Art, New York.
　　Gift of the artist. 1648.68.13a.

STEVEN SORMAN

American, born 1948

Spillville by Patricia Hampl
Minneapolis, Milkweed Editions, 1987
27 engravings, 12 × 17 inches each page
Edition 150
Courtesy Milkweed Editions, Minneapolis

DONALD SULTAN

American, born 1951

Warm and Cold by David Mamet
New York, Solo Press Inc. and Joe Fawbush Editions, 1985
9 lithographs with *pochoir* and letterpress,
　　21⅛ × 17⅛ inches each page
Edition 100
Courtesy Solo Press Inc., New York

Ancillary material:
Stencil for *pochoir* printing for *If You Are Far Away from Home
　　and A Keepsake Will Remind You of Those Who Love You*
20 × 24 inches
Courtesy Solo Press Inc., New York

ANTONI TÀPIES

Spanish, born 1923

Çà suit son cours by Edmond Jabès
Paris, Editions Fata Morgana, 1975
4 color etchings, 10¾ × 6¾ inches each page
Cover, inkless intaglio and etching, 10¾ × 6¾ inches
Edition 102
Courtesy Fundació Antoni Tàpies, Barcelona

JEAN TINGUELY

Swiss, born 1925

La Vittoria
Milan, Sergio Tosi Stampatore, 1970
31 mixed-media prints, 19¼ × 13⅝ inches each page
Edition 100
Courtesy Sergio Tosi, Paris and Rome

RICHARD TUTTLE

American, born 1941

Hiddenness by Mei-mei Berssenbrugge
New York, Library Fellows of the Whitney Museum
　　of American Art, 1987
4 handstamped prints, 15 × 10 inches each page
Edition 120
Collection Library of the Whitney Museum of
　　American Art, New York

Ancillary material:
4 hand-stamping tools used for *Hiddenness*, 1987
Dimensions variable
Courtesy of the artists

Preparatory drawing for *Hiddenness*
Gouache on paper, 15½ × 20½ inches
Courtesy of the artists

**SUSAN WEIL AND
MARJORIE VAN DYKE**

Americans, born 1930 and 1956

The Epiphanies by James Joyce
New York, Vincent Fitz Gerald & Co., 1987
64 mixed-media prints with hand work,
　　14 × 12 inches each page
Edition 50
Courtesy Vincent Fitz Gerald & Co., New York

Ancillary material:
Maquette for *Death* section, *The Epiphanies*, 1987
Watercolor (6 pages), 14 × 12 inches each page
Courtesy Vincent Fitz Gerald & Co., New York

Untitled (fish image), from *Death* section, *The Epiphanies*, 1987
Etching, 14 × 24 inches
Courtesy Vincent Fitz Gerald & Co., New York

Zinc plate, 16 × 24 inches
Courtesy Vincent Fitz Gerald & Co., New York

NEIL WELLIVER

American, born 1929

Henrik Ibsen, Poems translated by Michael Feingold
New York, Vincent Fitz Gerald & Co., 1987
1 lithograph, 5 etchings, 8½ × 11½ inches each page
Edition 75
Courtesy Vincent Fitz Gerald & Co., New York

Ancillary material:
Abraham Lincoln drawing, 3 copperplates, set of four tap outs,
　　and final print; 14 × 43¾ inches framed
Courtesy Vincent Fitz Gerald & Co., New York

WILLIAM T. WILEY

American, born 1937

Suite of Daze by William T. Wiley
Chicago, Landfall Press Inc., 1976
13 color intaglio prints, 16⅜ × 12⁹⁄₁₆ inches each page
Edition 50
Courtesy Landfall Press, Chicago and New York

Ancillary material:
Beginning Passes, from *Suite of Daze*, 1976
Aquatint and roulette, 16⅜ × 12⁹⁄₁₆ inches
Courtesy Landfall Press, Chicago and New York

Down the Line with Ol' Sir Rot, from *Suite of Daze*, 1976
Etching and roulette, 16⅜ × 12⁹⁄₁₆ inches
Courtesy Landfall Press, Chicago and New York

Hanging up the Frame, from *Suite of Daze*, 1976
Etching, 16⅜ × 12⁹⁄₁₆ inches
Courtesy Landfall Press, Chicago and New York

The Glittering Remains, from *Suite of Daze*, 1976
Etching, aquatint, and roulette, 16⅜ × 12⁹⁄₁₆ inches
Courtesy Landfall Press, Chicago and New York

Copperplate for *The Glittering Remains*, 13¹⁵⁄₁₆ × 10 inches
Courtesy Landfall Press, Chicago and New York

GLOSSARY

aquatint An intaglio process imitating the broad flat tints of watercolor or wash drawings achieved by etching a microscopic grain on the copper or zinc plate intended for printing.

Ben-Day The Ben-Day process is a method of laying a screen (dots, lines, and other textures) on art work or plates to obtain various tones and shadings. Similar effects can be produced by an artist working directly on the original artwork with a mechanical screen, a thin transparent film printed with white or black dots to simulate halftone work.

binding, accordion A method of binding a book so that the paper of which the pages are made is folded (or assembled) accordion fashion.

binding, French A method of binding in which all pages are double folded.

broadsheet (also known as **broadside**) A large un-divided sheet of paper printed on one side only, as for distribution or posting.

calligram A poem, printed in the shape of an object, in which the meaning of the poem relates to the object as it is drawn.

colophon A publisher or printer's distinctive emblem used as an identifying device on books, or an inscription generally found at the end of a manuscript or book, describing the particulars of an edition.

copperplate A plate of polished copper on which a picture, writing, or design is made by engraving or etching; a print or impression made from such a plate.

die-cutting A mechanical process of cutting regular or irregular shapes out of paper or other materials.

drypoint An intaglio process in which lines are cut into the surface of a plate with a pointed instrument such as a fine needle or a dental tool. (The surface of the plate is not prepared with a ground of any kind.) The cut of the needle creates a ridge of metal called a burr. In printing, the burr holds the ink and yields a soft, warm, velvety line.

duotone A method of printing an illustration either in a dark and a tinted shade of the same color or in two different colors from two plates of a monochrome original made from negatives at different screen angles.

embossing To raise or represent (surface designs) in relief; to decorate a surface with raised ornament; in metalwork, to raise a design on (a blank) with dies of a similar pattern on the negative of the other.

embossing, blind or **blind stamp** To emboss or impress the cover or spine of a book without using ink or foil (without the use of color).

engraving, line The earliest of the intaglio processes. The art of forming designs by incising the surface of a metal plate, block of wood, or the like, with a sharp, lozenge-shaped tool called a graver or burin, for the purpose of taking off impressions or prints of the design so formed. A **photo engraving** is classified as a line engraving (zinc or zinc etching) used for reproduction of material containing only solid blacks and whites.

etching An intaglio process of making designs or pictures on a metal plate, glass, etc., by the corrosive action of an acid instead of a burin. Etching can further be defined as an impression, as on paper, taken from an etched plate; a design produced by that method; or a metal plate bearing such a design.

etching, deep relief The process, in offset lithography, of making a working plate on which the image is etched very slightly below the nonprinting surface, giving fine detail.

etching, soft-ground A process in which an etching ground usually mixed with tallow, is used to create textural effects.

etching, sugar-lift A process is which an etching ground made of sugar, ink (litho or India), and water is drawn with a brush or pen onto a bare metal or aquatinted plate.

folio Paper folded once to make two leaves or four pages of a book; a volume having pages of the largest size, formerly made of such a sheet or a book made up of sheets folded only once; a leaf or page numbered only on the front side.

gatefold A foldout i.e., a page larger than the trim size of a book, folded one or more times so as not to extend beyond the book's pages.

golden-section A ratio between two portions of a line, or the two dimensions of a plane figure, in which the lesser of the two is to the greater as the greater is to the sum of both: a ratio of approximately 0.618 to 1.000; also called golden mean.

gutter The blank space or inner margin of a book, extending from the printing area to the binding.

handstamping The impression of a design or mark by hand.

intaglio The generic term for recessed printing tech-niques, including etching, engraving, aquatint, drypoint, and mezzotint. A process by which a design or text is incised into the surface of a plate so that, when ink is applied and excess wiped off, ink remains in the grooves and is transferred to paper under pressure in printing. Also, incised carving in relief ornamentation with a figure or design sunk below the surface.

letterpress The process of printing from raised surfaces, such as type, photoengravings, and wood or linoleum cuts. The paper is pressed against the inked surface to form an impression.

linocut A relief print made from a design cut into linoleum mounted on a block of wood.

lithography A planographic process, the key principle of which depends upon the antipathy of grease and water. The art of producing a picture, writing, or the like, on a flat specially-prepared limestone or aluminum plate, with some greasy or oily substance, and of taking ink impressions from this as in ordinary printing.

lithography, continuous-tone A photographic image which has not been screened and contains gradient tones from black to white.

lithography, offset An adaptation of the principles of stone lithography in which the design or page is photographically reproduced on a thin flexible metal plate. For photo-offset, a negative is used. If especially fine quality is wanted, a positive is used to prepare a deep-etch plate. The plate is curved to fit one of the revolving cylinders of the printing press. The design on this plate is transferred, or offset, on the paper by means of a rubber blanket that runs over another cylinder. Other terms for this process are planography and lithoprinting.

lithography, photo- The art of producing a lithograph printed from stone or the like upon which a picture or design has been formed by photography.

maquette A small model or study in three dimensions for either a sculptural or architectural project; a preliminary sketch.

mezzotint An intaglio process of engraving on copper or steel by burnishing or scraping away a uniformly roughened surface; a print produced by this method.

mylar sheets Sheets of a strong, thin polyester film used in photography.

off-register Register in printing is a) the precise adjustment or correspondence as of columns, lines, etc., on two sides of a leaf, or b) the correct relation, or exact superimposition, of colors in color printing. To register is to print an impression on a sheet in correct relationship to other impressions already printed on the same sheet, e.g., to superimpose exactly the various color impressions in process color printing. When such impressions are not exactly aligned, when the exact relationships are not in force, they are said to be off register, or out of register.

planography The art or technique of printing from a flat surface directly or by offset.

plate marks The imprint made on paper by the edges (usuallt bevelled) of a metal plate during printing.

pochoir A stencil for handcoloring.

proof An impression taken at any stage in the making of a print.

proof press, offset A small, hand-operated press for pulling proofs made by the offset process. See offset lithography.

relief printing Any printing process in which the printing ink is transferred to paper or another printed surface from areas that are higher than the rest of the block.

remarque A distinguishing mark or peculiarity indicating a particular stage of a plate; a small sketch engraved in the margin of a plate, and usually removed after a number of early proofs have been printed; or a plate so marked.

screenprint See silkscreen.

serigraph A print made by the silkscreen process.

silkscreen A printmaking technique in which a mesh cloth is stitched over a heavy wooden frame and the design, painted on the screen by tusche or affixed by stencil, is printed by having a squeegee force color through the pores of the material in areas not blocked out by a glue sizing; a print made by this technique.

thermography A technique for imitating an embossed appearance by dusting printed areas with a powder that adheres only to the wet ink, and fusing the ink and powder to the paper by heat.

tusche The liquid emulsion ink painted or drawn on a lithographic plate to form an image.

wood block A block of wood engraved in relief, for printing from; a print or impression made from such a block.

woodcut The oldest of all the printmaking processes. A relief-carved block of wood from which prints are made, or a print or impression from the raised areas of such a block.

INDEX

PUBLISHERS